School Personnel Systems

School Personnel Systems

Claude W. Fawcett
University of California

LexingtonBooks
D.C. Heath and Company
Lexington, Massachusetts
Toronto

Library of Congress Cataloging in Publication Data

Fawcett, Claude W.
School personnel systems.

Includes index.
1. School personnel management. I. Title
LB2831.5.F32 371.4 78-57240
ISBN 0-669-02375-2

Published simultaneously in Canada.

Printed in the United States of America.

International Standard Book Number: 0-669-02375-2

Library of Congress Catalog Card Number: 78-057240

To Mary Catherine

Mens sibi conscia recti.

Contents

	List of Figures and Tables	x
	Preface	xi
	Acknowledgments	xiii
Chapter 1	**The Personnel Service in Public School Systems**	1
	The Role of the Personnel Department	1
	Personnel Department Role Development in Business and Industry, Government, and Schools	1
	Styles of Administration	5
	Social Systems Administration	9
	The Role of the Personnel Department in Social Systems Administration	10
	Summary	12
Chapter 2	**The Personnel Department's Role in School Planning**	15
	Personnel Information Needed for Planning	15
	School System Planning	24
	Summary	29
Chapter 3	**Recruitment**	33
	Planning for Recruitment	34
	The General Market	39
	Evaluation of Sources of Supply	41
	Affirmative Action: Legal Bases and a Four-Step Model	42
	Recruitment Screening	45
	The Organization as a Market: Transfers	48
	Other Organizations as a Market: Cooperation among Districts	50
	Summary	52
Chapter 4	**Fine Screening: The Selection Process**	55
	Validation of Records	55
	Skills Confirmation	59
	Substantiation of Work Habits	61

	Candidate Reactions to Prior Assignments: The Patterned Interview	67
	Fine Screening Reports	70
	Summary	71
Chapter 5	**Assignment and Transfer**	73
	Scientific Administration Assignment Policies and Procedures	73
	Human Relations Administration Assignment Policies and Procedures	75
	Social System Administration Assignment Policies and Procedures	79
	Summary	88
Chapter 6	**Performance Appraisal**	91
	Scientific Management Techniques	91
	Human Relations Techniques	92
	Social Systems Evaluation Policies	93
	Social Systems Evaluation Procedures	95
	Obstacles to Adoption	99
	Summary	104
Chapter 7	**Human Resource Development**	107
	Clarification of Organizational Goals and Subgoals	109
	Development of Organizational Participation	113
	Organizational Commitment to Skill Development	117
	Organizational Reinforcement of Desirable Employee Behavior	122
	Summary	124
Chapter 8	**Collective Bargaining**	127
	Relations with the Negotiator	131
	Preparation for Bargaining	132
	Participation in Negotiations	136
	Contract Administration	138
	Summary	143
Chapter 9	**Compensation**	147
	Competitive Salaries	147
	Compensation Equity	150

Employee Benefits 158
Summary 165

Epilogue: The Dialogue of Change 169

Index 173

About the Author 177

List of Figures and Tables

Figures

7-1	Role Definitions: Management Responsibility Guide	112
7-2	Organizational Climate Survey	118
9-1	Suggested Salary Structure according to Achievement Classifications	153

Table

8-1	Data Needed for Collective Bargaining	135

Preface

This book expresses one man's faith in the teaching profession. If that faith is to be vindicated, teachers and students will share educational tasks they know are important. But tasks important to teachers and students may be considered routine by leaders of the myriad other groups that compete for students' learning time in a metroplitan community. Only concerted action by the people of a community can resolve the conflicts that arise over what should be learned in schools, other groups, or by the student himself. It is upon the resolution of these conflicts that teachers and students may be assured not only that their joint efforts are important, but that they will be supported by others in completing their tasks.

Yet, only a professional can help each student master the diverse and difficult learning tasks of a metropolitan society. And only the members of the profession, by their experimentation and exchange of results, can develop a common understanding of the skills of the profession, for it is the insightful use of proved skills in joint endeavors with students that gives to both groups the promise that their tasks will be completed with favorable results. Since professional teaching is done in schools, there is much that the school system can do to foster professional development.

The school system fosters professional development when it (1) selects teachers whose values, skills, and habits of work permit them to be colleagues of others in the school system; (2) assigns them to tasks that they value; (3) facilitates exchanges of expertise between colleagues; (4) maintains a challenging organizational climate that focuses on human resource development and prompt resolution of conflict; (5) pays equitable salaries; and (6) encourages teachers to make adequate provisions for retirement, health maintenance, legal obligations, and disasters of early demise or disability. These organizational services are commonly coordinated by the personnel department, which conducts them in the administrative style required by public opinion, the board of education, administrators present, and the kind of staff available.

Administration responsive to current political, economic, and social conditions will provide the personnel department the greatest opportunity to foster professional growth. These conditions are readily identified. The many groups pressuring to fill the learning time of students in a metropolitan community force the use of some method of defining the role of the school. Teachers are products of many subcultures and prior experiences; they display unique skills and insights. This diversity may be an asset in an institution that accepts children and youth from many subcultures. The administration that can coordinate the efforts of a diverse staff in a multicultural community—and insist only that the proved professional skills be used to achieve agreed-upon goals—is called, in today's terminology, social systems coordination.

And it is this style of administration that has changed the role of the personnel department from record-keeping, recruiting, and welfare administration to policymaking, resource development, and conflict resolution. In so doing, it has changed the role of the personnel administrator from staff spokesman for the employees to top-level consultant on the maintenance of a favorable organizational climate. It is an organizational role that requires him to report directly to the top administrator. This book was written in expectation that the inexorable demands of a metropolitan culture will require personnel administrators to meet the demands of the new role.

Acknowledgments

This book is a synthesis of ideas provided by many people. Personnel planning recommendations were the product not only of experience as a secondary school principal and school superintendent, but of membership in the UCLA Budget Council and the University of California Educational Policies Committee. Aubrey Berry, a colleague during my seven years of service as the UCLA Educational Placement Officer, provided many ideas about recruitment. Selection recommendations were strongly influenced by Robert N. McMurry, whose firm, the McMurry Company, once recommended me for an executive position in a national association of manufacturers. The assignment problems of role definition and conflict resolution were underlined by Robert D. Melcher of the Management Guidance Corporation during years of friendship and collaboration. Garth Sorenson, a UCLA colleague, provided the idea for performance appraisal by insisting that evaluation was a process of determining the presence or absence of expected behavior. Clarence Fielstra, another UCLA colleague, provided insights concerning personnel development. Collective bargaining ideas were products of my service as an arbitrator. Compensation ideas came from experience as a school administrator and from other administrators during consultation with them about personnel problems. But the ideas concerning administrative theory stemmed from other sources.

I am indebted to Robert J. Havighurst, University of Chicago, for insights concerning the community's role in education; to Harry Broudy, University of Illinois, for an exposition of the uncertain role of the schools in today's culture; to Milton J. Rokeach, Washington State University, for a usable concept of value consensus; and to Philip J. Selznick, University of California, for an understanding of the role of values in staff motivation. But these ideas came to full meaning when used as a part of school administration theory.

Comparisons of school administration theories were made possible by references to the writings of Ellwood P. Cubberley, Kurt Lewin, Frederick J. Taylor, Franklin Bobbitt, George Strayer, John Dewey, and Francis Spaulding. Reliance was placed on the ideas of Rensis Likert, University of Michigan, and Cyril Sofer, Cambridge University, in adapting social systems coordination to public school administration. But the many graduate students inquiring with me about school administration theories in graduate seminars for the past eighteen years have done most to provide form and substance to the ideas of this book.

I am indebteded to Sipora Gruskin, editorial consultant, for advice concerning matters of form and style; to Bill Fulton for artwork; and to Barbara Thompson for typing of the manuscript.

1 The Personnel Service in Public School Systems

The Role of the Personnel Department

The common role of the personnel department in a public school system may be described as providing guidance in securing, developing, and retaining individuals who possess or are able to obtain the skills, attitudes, and knowledge essential to the achievement of the community's goals of education. Foulkes and Morgan described these functions as follows:

> The "bread and butter" of the personnel job is service to line management. Personnel assists in the hiring, training, rewarding, counseling, promoting, and firing of employees at all levels. Personnel administers the various benefits programs such as educational reimbursement, health and accident programs, retirement, vacation, and sick leave. The department has a role with respect to grievances.[1]

These authors' somewhat pragmatic definition may be a bit sophisticated for middle-sized and smaller school districts, particularly those in which administrators carry on the personnel function without much professional guidance. However, their description accurately reflects the functions of the personnel department in the larger school districts in metropolitan centers.

Briefly, then, personnel administration in public school systems may be identified three ways: (1) as a staff function; (2) as a skilled professional activity; and (3) as an integral part of the goal accomplishment process of a public school system.

The development of this personnel department role in metropolitan school districts, though now similar to the role of personnel departments in business and industry as well as government, followed a different and tortuous path.

Personnel Department Role Development in Business and Industry, Government, and Schools

Business and Industry

In 1964, Wendell French attributed the development of modern personnel management in business and industry to six interrelated sources:

Rapid technological change and specialization beginning with the Industrial Revolution;

The emergence of free collective bargaining;

The scientific management movement;

Early industrial psychology;

The emergence of personnel specialists, including employment agents, welfare secretaries, wage clerks, safety directors, the industrial physician, and the consolidation of all of these into a personnel department; and

The human relations movement.[2]

In line with today's requirements, French might well have added a seventh—social systems demands of public responsibility, affirmative action, equal rights, and equal compensation.

The Government

The Federal Civil Service Act of 1883, which formed the civil service system, is still operating in most governments. The major tenets of personnel management within this system may be listed as follows:

Competitive examinations.

Group interviewing and rating for many positions by committees.

Establishment of a list of eligibles in the order of rating.

Credit (often) for military service in calculating scores.

Permanence after a reasonably short probationary period.

Grievance hearing by the appointed Civil Service Board.

Civil service commissions and boards are appointed by the political structure in power. It is fair to say, then, that most appointive positions, whether in federal, state, local, town, county, or city governments, are filled by the civil service system.

If the personnel department's role in government came about as an attempt to secure efficient employees in the face of political pressures to appoint friends of elected officials, in business and industry, the role developed not only to find the right man for the job, but to secure employee cooperation and identification with the organization. The role of the personnel department in public school systems developed in a different manner.

Public School Systems

At one time, when schools were neighborhood enterprises conducted by local boards of education, the members of these boards assumed strict administrative responsibility for the certification, appointment, and termination of all personnel—teaching and nonteaching. Of these, the first power relinquished was certification, which was given to town or county educational authorities to facilitate interdistrict movement of personnel. As mobility of teachers became more customary and desirable, the certification power was assumed by the state education authority. School boards' powers to select and terminate were jealously guarded until compassion for the superintendent's need to work with appointed people led to their delegation to him—but the boards firmly retained the power of veto over both functions.

This sharing of responsibility for selection and termination generated a precarious personnel situation. Often the superintendent's position was uncertain, and frequently unpredictable decisions were reached by boards of education. Teachers and school administrators began to develop plans that incorporated personnel rules and regulations into state laws. Under state powers of certification, requirements for licenses were written into statutes. In some instances this created new problems. In California, for example, by 1961 there were forty-eight different licenses—supplemented by nineteen special certificates. Further, state minimal salaries were designated. Retirement systems were established with elaborate qualification and contribution requirements. Tenure provisions became a part of statutes. Termination procedures were incorporated into the education code. Sometimes, inservice requirements for license renewals were legislated. In addition to these state actions, the single salary schedule was adopted almost universally. This provided for almost automatic salary progression based on length of service and academic (inservice) credits earned. No major intervention of administrative evaluation was necessary. As a result of these legislated and voluntary administrative procedures, the personnel process within school districts was minimized.

This convenient reliance on the state for establishment of personnel policies was challenged by the events of the decade and a half following 1957 (the year of the Russian *Sputnik*). School districts became large public enterprises; their numbers decreased from 52,943 in 1957 to 17,238 in 1972.[3] Elementary and secondary school enrollments increased from 32,334,000 in 1957 to 47,002,000 in 1972.[4] The teaching staff increased from 1,205,000 in 1957 to 2,187,000 in 1972.[5] Post-*Sputnik* concern for the development of scientists and engineers brought an ever increasing demand for accountability in public education. The burgeoning approval of collective bargaining for public employees began in earnest with President Kennedy's Executive Order 10988 of 1962, establishing "meet and confer" policies for consulting with unions of government workers. The Civil Rights Act of 1964 included Title VII, which forbids discrimination in employment. All of these events created pressures on school districts to develop personnel policies and practices indigenous to the employing unit. However, the most immediate and powerful need was to find and employ an additional million teachers to be drawn from a short supply and to do so within the space of fifteen years—nearly a doubling of the teaching force.

In an attempt at meeting this problem, school superintendents turned to the remedy that had worked in prior periods of teacher shortage: the creation of personnel departments oriented primarily to the selection of personnel. The Dallas Independent School District, for example, had established in 1919, according to Harold Moore, the first public school personnel department during the shortage following World War I.[6] Greene, in commenting on Moore's estimate of 250 personnel departments in public school systems in 1966, reported that, by 1971, the total had risen to 750.[7] Both Moore and Greene suggested that this rapid growth was, in part, due to the shortages of teaching personnel following 1960. Even though the impetus for their creation was provided by superintendents desperately seeking staff, it was fortunate they were in place to cope with other personnel issues that arose between 1960 and 1979. These issues were:

Collective bargaining for teachers and other school employees, an almost universal phenomenon.

Demands of the public for accountability, lately much increased in number and intensity.

Growth in size and complexity of school districts everywhere.

Repeated demands for changes in curriculum, organization, and cooperative relations with other community institutions.

The need for programs endorsed by federal and state governments for integration, affirmative action, equal compensation, and equal personnel treatment.

There can be no doubt that all these crucial—and current—problems had a direct impact on the school systems' personnel policies and procedures. It would seem evident that nothing less than a sophisticated department, staffed by skilled personnel administrators, could provide the services required.

The sophistication required of personnel administrators may die aborning unless it can be developed within a compatible style of district administration. Because most public school systems today are administered by so-called scientific management policies, amended only to a degree by policies originating in human relations theories, an examination of options may contribute to some estimate of the most favorable administrative climate for the development of modern educational personnel policies and practices.

Styles of Administration

1. Since it is still the prime determinant of school administration policies, the first option that should be examined is the style of management named "scientific administration" by Supreme Court Justice Brandeis. Borrowed from practices of business and industry, it was a management approach fully endorsed by the first schools to prepare school administrators. Cubberly of Stanford summarized scientific administration as follows:

> The specifications for manufacturing come from the demands of twentieth century civilization, and it is the business of the school to build its pupils according to the specifications laid down. This demands good tools, specialized machinery, continuous measurement of production to see if it is according to specifications, the elimination of waste in manufacturing, and a large variety in output.[8]

From the vantage point of today, it seems fair to say that the statement would have been endorsed, in part or in whole, by Franklin Bobbitt of the University of Chicago, George Strayer of Teachers College, Columbia University, and Francis Spaulding of Yale University. They might have agreed, also, with the following Cubberly statement about the policymaking powers of school executives:

> As the executive officer of the board of education and the chief executive of the school system, the superintendent plays a somewhat different role. Both by law and by the rules and regulations of the board he has little authority, except in matters in which the board has seen fit to delegate authority to him, yet he will not be of much force as a superintendent unless he can come to exercise rather larger powers.[9]

Cubberly further suggested how the superintendent could use research, persuasion, and appeals to the community if he wished for the board of education to delegate powers to him.

2. Considering the autocratic approach to management and policy-making in schools run on these notions of unity of command, separation of policy and execution, and bureaucratic planning, it is not surprising to find it challenged, in the 1930s and 1940s, by those who believed in democracy in group operations. It is an administrative style named the "human

relations" approach. Among the educators who sponsored this type of management, possibly the most significant were Kurt Lewin of the Massachusetts Institute of Technology and John Dewey of Teachers College, Columbia University. In commenting on their support for democracy in administration, Gordon Allport said:

> There is a striking kinship between the work of Kurt Lewin and the work of John Dewey. Both agree that democracy must be learned anew in each generation, and that it is a far more difficult form of social structure to attain and to maintain than is autocracy. Both see intimate dependence of democracy upon social science. Without knowledge of, and obedience to, the laws of human nature in group settings, democracy cannot succeed. And without freedom for research and theory as provided only in a democratic environment social science will surely fail. Dewey, we might say, is the outstanding philosophical exponent of democracy, Lewin is its outstanding psychological exponent. More clearly than anyone else has he shown us in concrete, operational terms what it means to be a democratic leader, and to create a democratic group structure.[10]

In a search of a definition of the human relations administrator, great emphasis was placed on his role as a "facilitator" of group activity. Cartwright and Zander described this administrative role as follows:

> Examples of member behaviors that serve functions of goal achievement are "initiates action," "keeps member's attention on goals," "clarifies issues," "develops a procedural plan," "evaluates the quality of work done," and "makes expert information available." Examples of behaviors that serve functions of group maintenance are "keeps interpersonal relations pleasant," "arbitrates disputes," "provides encouragement," "gives the minority a chance to be heard," "stimulates self direction," and "increases interdependence among members."[11]

Despite universal endorsement of the idea of organizational democracy, school administrators found it difficult, if not impossible, to initiate more than the forms of democratic administration. They created many consultative committees; they sponsored group activities—including faculty and other group meetings, the district bowling leagues, social gatherings, and other events intended to foster member interdependence. But they retained the concepts of chain of command, delegation of authority, bureaucratic planning, and the power to veto group decisions. Perhaps there were no other alternatives in a society committed to the principles of accountability and efficiency. And it must be pointed out here that these same societal demands—accentuated by the problems of metropolitanization—today stand in the way of the newer administrative adjustments that must be made to facilitate the effective coordination of educational activities in a society composed of many, often conflicting, social groups.

3. To meet the needs of today, there is a new approach to administrative thought, one that is often termed "social systems administration." In it, the school system is considered but a subsystem of a larger community social system, and its role is determined in concert with the roles of other subsystems. Further, its role determines the goals of its activities. Subgoals are assigned to educational employees as tasks that are a part of role definition. In this view, all members of the workforce, including administrators, are colleagues with well-defined roles in the completion of tasks. It is assumed that each workforce participant is commited to achieving his portion of the group task. Here, administration is considered to be a process of coordinating the collegial goal accomplishment effort of many diverse people. It is a concept of administration so far removed from the tenets of scientific administration that it is small wonder school administrators were, at times, deluded into embracing modernized versions of both the scientific management and the human relations approach. Before elaborating on social systems administration, these enthusiastic, if not wholly successful attempts at revival of older systems of administrative action must be discussed.

Enthusiasm No. 1: Neoscientific Management

The development of computers, with their facility for storage, retrieval, and quick manipulation of data, lent a new credence to the notions of scientific administration. Even conglomerates and large organizations were said to be able to manage the information exchange problems essential to bureaucratic coordination. A number of popular acronyms appeared: PERT (Program Evaluation and Review Technique), CPM (Critical Path Method, used with PERT), PPBS (Program Planning and Budgeting System). There were, as well, endless systems models and modeling. But when the enthusiasm for neoscientific administration led to experimentation, it was found that this approach, like its original, relied ultimately on a stable, relatively independent, bureaucratic organization for success—a type of organization largely outdated in a complex, interdependent, metropolitan society. The neoscientific approach constituted only one type of experimentation that was developed because of social pressures. Another experiment was a revival of the human relations type of management.

Enthusiasm No. 2: Neohuman Relations Approach

The most common form of neohumanism was the self-managed group. This reached its maximum development to date in some Swedish manufacturing companies. President Gyllenhammar of the Volvo Corporation detailed his firm's use of self-managed groups in a 1977 issue of the *Harvard Business Review.*[12] It has not been a notably successful effort in the American firms that experimented with it. The nearest approach to this concept in terms of public school administration was the decentralization of curriculum determination and community relations and their delegation to individual schools. However, few principals either possessed the understanding of the process or had the freedom from central office influence to build a truly self-managed group. Despite its obvious intellectual and emotional appeal to those committed to pure democracy, its lack of utility may be ascribed to its inability to cope with the interdependent social relations characteristic of modern metropolitan activities. Still, despite the weaknesses inherent in both neoscientific and neohuman administrative practices, some nationally known professors of school administration did recommend their use in a bimodal system of school management.

Enthusiasm No. 3: Bimodal Neoscientific and Neohumanistic Administration

Morphet, Johns, and Reller defined the bimodal use of neoscientific and neohumanism administration as follows:

> The emerging pluralistic, collegial concept of organization can best be described as a modification of the monocratic, bureaucratic concept, providing for a pluralistic sharing of power to make policy and program decisions on a collegial basis. Under this concept, the organization is structured hierarchically, as in Weber's bureaucracy, to implement programs and policy, and is structured collegially on an egalitarian basis for making policy and program decisions.[13]

The bimodal view of administration failed to recognize the inherent conflict that persists between the bureaucratic system and the employee—and the subsequent necessity to cope with it. Also ignored, or not taken into account, were the possibility of multigroup loyalties, growing employee sophistication, and the social impact of organizational activity. This amalgamation of two only partially effective systems hardly produced a result better than either.

Although these attempts at revival of older systems of administrative action did not really succeed, they served a useful purpose. They pointed up the need for a modernized system responsive to the social, economic, and political context of the day. The social systems style of management may prove to be the solution.

Social Systems Administration

Based on these multiple concepts of the school as a subsystem of the larger community social system, the collegiality of all participants, the necessity of role clarification, and administration as coordinating the work of many diverse persons seeking a common goal, participants in the social system approach are recognized as members of many social groups and partners in decision-making. They are recognized as unified by value consensus and technical competence.

Young noted how social systems administration rejected the bureaucracy as the center of administrative attention, as follows:

> What appears to be occurring is that our conception of organization is changing from one of structure to one of process. Rather than visualize the organization in its traditional structural, bureaucratic, and hierarchical motif with a fixed set of authority relationships much like the scaffolding of a building, we are beginning now to view organizations as a set of flows, information, men, material, and behavior. Time and change are critical aspects.[14]

Miles applied this systems concept to schools:

> [Schools are] a bounded collection of interdependent parts, devoted to the accomplishment of some goal or goals, with the parts maintained in a steady state of relation to each other and the environment by means of (1) standard modes of operation, and (2) feedback from the environment about the consequences of system actions.[15]

Kluckhohn pointed out that goals are the product of a dynamic consensus of beliefs, attitudes, and values:

> A value is a conception, explicit or implicit, distinctive of an individual or characteristic of a group, of the desirable which influences the selection from available modes, means, and ends of action. . . . This definition takes culture, group, and the individual's relation to culture and place in his group as primary points of departure.[16]

Perhaps the clearest definition of social systems administration was given by Brooks Adams in 1914 when he described administration as "the ability to coordinate many, often conflicting, social energies so adroitly that they operate as a unity."[17]

The development of a social systems style of administration may be said to expand and redirect the activities of the personnel department. In social systems administration, recruitment under scientific management and facilitation under human relations are modified to mean human resource development. This new responsibility demands an examination of the parameters of a new and expanded role for the personnel department.

The Role of the Personnel Department in Social Systems Administration

Organizational Planning

In social systems administration, the personnel department becomes one of the most important sources of information in the setting of organizational goals and the adoption of operational policies. In establishing goals for the public schools, it is the personnel department that can, and should, provide an accurate inventory of skills available among persons employed. It should also provide the most recent information concerning personnel attitudes (motivation) for the accomplishment of such goals. The department possesses the most accurate inventory of knowledge possessed by the working staff. It should, therefore, be asked to indicate whether skills, attitudes, and knowledge lacking in the staff are in supply—and the extent of the supply—in the market area from which personnel are selected. If the staff is deficient and the market supply problematic, the department should be asked to estimate the pre- and inservice education required to make it possible to assemble an effective staff within a designated time. It would seem that public schools' goal formulation without these data amounts to a prayer or, possibly, a public relations device to ease tension in a demand situation.

But the personnel department's role in organizational planning extends beyond providing such feasibility data. It should include participation in policy formulation, most specifically because policies are adopted to foster coordination of work among diverse departments and employees. Foulkes and Morgan quoted Edwin H. Land, chief executive officer of the Polaroid Corporation, on one such policy. Land explained a Polaroid policy as follows:

> [The other] is to give everyone working for the company a personal opportunity within the company for full exercise of his talents—to express his opinions, to share in the progress of the company as far as his capacities permit, and to earn enough money so that the need for earning more will not always be the first thing on his mind. The opportunity, in short, to make his work here a fully rewarding and important part of his life.[18]

In other words, this policy emphasizes human resource development, which, in social systems administration, is typically allocated to the personnel department for oversight.

If these planning tasks are to be completed effectively, the personnel department should be assigned a major role in the planning/operating activities of the organization. And this recognition of leadership should extend to the department's services to administrators.

Service to Administrators

The personnel department has characteristically served administrators by participating in recruiting, selecting, orienting, assigning, evaluating, retraining, paying, counseling, terminating, and retiring members of the workforce. It has learned to cooperate with many types of administrators, with individual styles as well as different administrative postures and techniques. But whatever the style, the personnel department has encouraged, helped, developed, and challenged administrators to make the best use of staff talents. In social systems administration, participation includes not only direct cooperative activities with administrators, but also the formulation of operating policies and frequent audits of procedures adopted to implement policies.

Audits conducted by the personnel department should include studies of administrators' relations with personnel, surveys of markets, attitudinal surveys, wage and salary studies, skill inventories, retention and turnover, benefits paid as salary, management skills within the workforce, and effectiveness of inservice programs. These data can be used to recommend new, or modify old, operational policies, but their chief use is to challenge administrators to review the effectiveness of their relations with personnel. And they can be used to provide insight concerning the solutions of perplexing personnel problems.

Complex personnel problems do continue to arise as the result of governmental, union, or societal action. For example, if the legal requirements of affirmative action require the wholesale transfer of personnel, the feasibility of alternative solutions should be studied in the light of data supplied by the personnel department. If morale problems have interrupted organizational cooperation, personnel surveys should allow the identification of the location and source of the difficulty. If salaries are inadequate, the nature of a competitive salary policy should be provided by the personnel department. All these are essential obligations in a personnel department's service to administrators. However, even though they constitute the largest block of tasks assigned within the role of the personnel department, another substantial block is composed of tasks concerned with employee relations.

Employee Relations

Employee relations tasks of the personnel department have multiplied as the result of collective bargaining. The acceptance of the procedure as a means of resolving economic conflicts between the district and the employees has added negotiations to the tasks of the personnel department. This has required the addition of special skills to the department—including negotiating, wage and salary determination, conduct of grievance proceedings, and administration of employee benefits programs. Because collective bargaining developed as an adversarial contest, early experience in the private sector often brought the notion that negotiating skills were incompatible with personnel administration. However, later experience showed that good personnel practices—particularly practices endorsed by social systems concepts—were able to reduce the extent of conflict sufficiently to make the limited capacity of negotiations for reconciling conflicts more effective. In any case, the addition of these employee relations tasks can be made less onerous by the allocation of human resource development responsibilities to the personnel department.

Human Resource Development

Other areas of leadership of the personnel department include the maintenance of organizational health, the development of inservice development programs that supplement the coaching process inherent in evaluation, organizational development, and organizational identification and participation. Unlike the European concept of codetermination, which elevates employee interests to a par with stockholder interests, the social systems concept of human resource development places emphasis on collegiality in the accomplishment of commonly accepted goals. This uniquely American definition of human resource development, therefore, gives the personnel department the task of overseeing organizational adaptation to individuals who work within an organization that has multiple relations with other community institutions.

Summary

The personnel service in a public school system can be identified as (1) a staff function, (2) a skilled professional activity, and (3) an integral part of the goal accomplishment process of a public school system. The service, though currently similar to that provided in other governments and in public sector organizations, developed in a different manner. At one time most significant personnel policies and practices were incorporated into state laws and the service in local school districts was minimized. State controls of public school personnel administration have slowly been remanded to local districts as the result of the advent of collective bargaining, increased size of school districts, and the development of a competent corps of personnel administrators. Their expanded responsibilities require the development of a personnel service with a consistent and appropriate style of administration. In the social, political, and economic parameters of today's society, this style seems likely to be a "social systems administration."

The role of the personnel department in a social systems administrative policy designates it as one of the most significant resources in the development of policies and procedures. Personnel services cooperate with administrators in recruiting, selecting, orienting, assigning, evaluating, developing, terminating, transferring, and retiring personnel. The personnel department takes a position of leadership in regard to employee relations that involve negotiations, wage and salary determination, conduct of grievance procedures, and the administration of benefits programs. Personnel also assumes leadership in human resource development, including the maintenance of organizational health, inservice training, organizational development, and employee identification with the organization.

Notes

1. Fred K. Foulkes and Henry M. Morgan, "Organizing and Staffing the Personnel Function," *Harvard Business Review* 55 (1977):146.
2. Wendell French, *The Personnel Management Process: Human Resources Administration* (Boston: Houghton Mifflin, 1964), pp. 19-20.
3. U.S. Bureau of the Census, *Statistical Abstract of the United States: 1961,* 82d ed. (Washington, D.C.: The Bureau, 1961), p. 401; U.S. Bureau of the Census, *Statistical Abstract of the United States: 1976,* 97th ed. (Washington, D.C.: The Bureau, 1976), p. 257.
4. U.S. Bureau of the Census, *1961 Statistical Abstract,* p. 115; U.S. Bureau of the Census, *1976 Statistical Abstract,* p. 119.
5. U.S. Bureau of the Census, *1961 Statistical Abstract,* p. 114; U.S. Bureau of the Census, *1976 Statistical Abstract,* p. 129.
6. Quoted by Jay Greene in *School Personnel Administration* (New York: Chilton, 1971), pp. 2-3.
7. Ibid., p. 4.
8. Ellwood Cubberley, *Public School Administration* (Boston: Houghton Mifflin, 1929), p. 512.
9. Ibid., p. 241.

10. Gordon W. Allport, "Foreward," in Kurt Lewin, *Resolving Social Conflicts*, ed. Gertrud Weiss Lewin (New York: Harper and Brothers, 1948), p. xi.

11. Dorwin Cartwright and Alvin Zander, eds., *Group Dynamics Research and Theory,* 2d ed. (Evanston, Ill.: Row, Peterson and Company, 1960), p. 496.

12. Pehr G. Gyllenhammar, "How Volvo Adapts Work to People," *Harvard Business Review* 55 (1977):102-113.

13. Edgar L. Morphet, Roe L. Johns, and Theodore L. Reller, *Educational Organization and Administration,* 3d ed. (Englewood Cliffs, N.J.: Prentice-Hall, 1974), p. 109.

14. Stanley Young, "Organization as a Total System," in *Systems, Organizations, Analyses, Management: A Book of Readings,* ed. Donald I. Cleland and William R. King (New York: McGraw-Hill, 1969), p. 51.

15. Matthew B. Miles, *Innovation in Education* (New York: Bureau of Publications, Teachers College, Columbia University, 1964), p. 13.

16. Clyde Kluckhohn, "Values and Value Orientations in the Theory of Action," in *Toward a General Theory of Action,* ed. Talcott Parsons and Edward A. Shils (Cambridge: Harvard University Press, 1951), p. 395.

17. Brooks Adams, *The Theory of Social Revolutions* (New York: Macmillan, 1914).

18. Foulkes and Morgan, "Organizing and Staffing the Personnel Function," p. 147.

2 The Personnel Department's Role in School Planning

Administrators subscribing to scientific and human relations administrative practices have assigned a post facto role to the personnel department in planning. The scientific approach makes no call upon personnel's professional expertise in policy formation and planning; the human relations approach only calls upon this expertise to provide compatible people after the policies have been adopted and the plans completed.

It would appear that this cavalier—if not wasteful—use of one of the organization's most crucial resources may well be counterproductive to the fulfillment of administration's major function: to recognize changing conditions and decide what to do about them. In this context, it is relevant to remember John Gardner's observation that the greatest barriers to change are to be found in the minds of men.[1] It is evident that timely and appropriate policies adopted by management can be ignored, or modified, by the neglect, opposition, or even sabotage of an unsympathetic or unknowing workforce. However magnificent the plans developed by management look on paper, lackadaisical or antagonistic actions by employees can frustrate even the best.

It follows that the ability of the school system to react to cultural change generally translates as a problem of modification of staff values and attitudes. This suggests that management's thorough knowledge of staff is critical to planning. It would seem appropriate to consider the personnel department as a vital and indispensable resource for effective organizational planning.

Personnel Information Needed for Planning

Full participation of the personnel department in planning, however, depends upon the organization's valuing its human resources as capital and assigning the task of monitoring human resource development to the personnel department. The former is one of the premises of social systems administration. The latter requires full organizational cooperation in the accumulation of data about personnel. Such data should include behavior of each employee as a member of many groups, informal and formal, within and without the school system; characteristic work habits; belief systems; precedents accepted and rejected; attitudes displayed in different group roles; identification with different groups; and characteristic interactions with others in them.

Of course, the accumulation of these data should be done according to the rules generally governing the use of all personnel files: with the full knowledge and cooperation of the employees. And, during the years the files are built up, legal and prudent procedures should have been observed. Among these procedures the following bear repeating. During his years of employment with the organization, the employee should have had access to his file and the opportunity to include extensions, rebuttals, or denials in his own words. He should have been encouraged to accept responsibility for initiating the incorporation of significant new data or the deletion of old or erroneous material. Any addition or deletion from the file not executed by him should have been brought immediately to his attention. He should have been assured that personnel files are made available only to responsible persons, whose interest and use of the files are directly related to organizational purposes. In other words, he should always consider the file his, its availability and up-to-dateness important to assist in the best utilization of his services within the system.

Thus the use of these complete files should enable the personnel administrator to provide educational planners with pertinent information not otherwise obtainable. If used properly, planners will have data concerning the following:

1. Skills available throughout the entire school system or in any segment thereof.
2. Work habits characteristic of each employee.
3. Educational belief systems of each employee.
4. Precedents, both honored and rejected.
5. Interaction patterns with other employees in different kinds of groups.

Delivery of these data to planners by the personnel department will be simplified if modern information storage systems are used and retrieval can be made with dispatch on call.

These five categories of specific personnel information, then, are determinants of the feasibility of organizational change as indicated by the following analyses.

1. Available Skills

It seems self-evident that any assignment created by a contemplated change should be filled with a person possessing the skills necessary to complete the intended work, but attempting to define these necessary skills for teachers is no simple task. Harry Broudy, in discussing the public schools' loss of credibility, had this to say about the complex nature of teaching skills: "There is virtually no consensus on procedures such as are found in carpentry, plumbing, law, medicine, accounting, or architecture. On the contary, the more idiosynchratically a teacher behaves, the more likely is he or she to be praised as innovative, imaginative, or ingenious."[2] Broudy continued: "Although public school teaching is a profession by rhetorical courtesy, and although academicians have some difficulty in playing the role of priestly intercessionaries for people desperately seeking to be saved from ignorance, the public still regards teaching as a redemptive calling and invests the educational establishment with a commitment to the pupil and the public good."[3]

Thus Broudy revived the concept of the priestly role of the teacher, early described by Charlemagne as "all those who by God's help are able to teach."[4] If this exalted view of the teacher were persistent, it would be impossible to compile a skill inventory. Nor can such an inventory be made from the competency- (or performance-) based lists advocated by some educational enthusiasts. These lists are composed of teaching acts rather than teaching skills. C. Michael Darcy provided an example of one such list, as follows:

001.0 Planning to Meet the Educational Needs of All Children

001.1 The administrator will list, or present a list prepared at his direction, the types of educational needs present among the students for which he is responsible.

001.2 The administrator will list, or present a list prepared at his direction, for each educational need presented above, a possible program, teaching strategy, or other process for meeting these needs.

001.3 The administrator will gather, or cause to be gathered, evidence as to the desirability of each process listed.

001.4 The administrator will explore, and prepare a report on the feasibility of, each recommended process.

001.5 Within the limits of feasibility as described under 001.4, the administrator will implement, or cause to be implemented, programs to meet the needs.

001.6 Included in the implementation of programs for meeting the educational needs of children will be evaluation procedures.

001.7 At appropriate intervals the administrator will evaluate the programs for meeting the educational needs of children.

001.8 The administrator will disseminate to the students, parents, and faculty the results, both favorable and unfavorable, of his plans.[5]

Clearly, if a skills inventory is to be useful to planners, it must be stated in terms of procedures endorsed by the profession, not action patterns listed by some person (or persons) within the profession.

Despite the reluctance of the profession to endorse them, as noted by Broudy, the skills of teaching are neither mysterious nor uncommon. In a study of teaching skills for the UCLA Graduate School of Education Ford Foundation Teacher Education Project, Fawcett in 1965 identified three major groups of teaching skills: (1) classroom management; (2) teacher-student interactions; and (3) educational process.[6] Although a number of skills were identified per group, three are used here to illustrate each category.

> For Classroom Management: challenging each different kind of student in class to develop personal learning goals; assisting each student to use the most economical learning procedures to reach his learning goals; and assisting each student to develop the capability for evaluating his learning progress.
>
> For Teacher-Student Interaction: reconciliation of the teacher's and students' needs for security in the learning process; reconciliation of the teacher's and students' needs for recognition; and reconciliation of the teacher's and students' needs for power in the classroom.
>
> For the Educational Process: use of tools and materials of instruction; diagnosis of learning difficulties of each student; and sequencing of instruction for each different kind of student in class.

These skills have the same kind of universality that one finds in carpentry when it is determined that a cabinetmaker can form a mortised joint, or in medicine when it is known that a surgeon can perform a heart bypass operation. These are the kinds of skills that can be observed, recorded, and reported. They are also the skills that must be considered in the context of contemplating organizational change.

2. Work Habits

Planners should receive information from the personnel department concerning the persistent and recurring work habits of employees. These include data concerning absenteeism under the manifold categories of leave available in most school districts (for example, sickness, maternity, personal, opportunity, military, sabbatical, and bereavement). McMurry recommended the inclusion of data concerning the psychic energy level, the tolerance of frustration, and the levels of aspiration.[7] He further suggested such information could be reported in terms of behavior related to observed work experiences.

But it is the employee as a member of the group that produces particularly pertinent data. Sofer isolated this group-individual aspect by adding an emotional dimension to work habits. He pointed out:

> No work group will keep consistently to its task. Each will alternate instead between the manifest tasks and what would appear from the outside to be emotional interferences with the real work. However described by members, the sources of this interference will be largely in their own interaction, including the hopes and disappointments of members concerning each other.[8]

It would seem imperative, then, to provide data that give evidence of characteristic interactions of employees within a group. McMurry suggested a breakdown of the data that would give some insight into the individual's "motives" in group interaction. He listed:

> The need for income;
>
> Security at work;
>
> Status in the organization;
>
> Power in the group;
>
> Curiosity;
>
> Creativity;
>
> The need to excel; and
>
> The need to serve.[9]

Two other dimensions of work habits were added by William Schutz and his collaborators in a study of California school administrators. In studying coping mechanisms, they noted that the rejection of the problem was manifested by (1) denial that a problem exists; (2) intellectual recognition of the problem without acceptance; (3) identification of the problem as belonging to someone else; (4) insistence of a need for more experience before attempting problem resolution; (5) self-accusation of full responsibility; and (6) rationalization of the problem into one that no one can solve.[10] A reciprocal dimension of the Schutz findings consisted of information concerning the employee's characteristic acceptance of the problem and examined the extent of rational use of orderly problem-solving skills.

It is difficult to assess the impact of persistent work habits on the possibility of organizational change, unless such habits are examined within a context of employees' educational belief systems.

3. Educational Belief Systems

If school employees are to coordinate their efforts in a group successfully, it would seem necessary that an educational values consensus broad enough to motivate joint effort be in existence. Data concerning educational values and their related attitudes should, therefore, be provided by the personnel department to facilitate decisions about organizational change. The importance of this kind of information to planning can be inferred from Rokeach's definition of beliefs. He defined values as follows:

> To say that a person has a value is to say that he has an enduring prescriptive or proscriptive belief that a specific mode of behavior or end-state of existence is preferred to an opposite mode of behavior or end-state. This belief transcends attitudes toward objects and toward situations; it is a standard that guides and determines action, attitudes toward objects and situations, ideology, presentations of self to others, evaluations, judgments, justifications, comparisons of self with others, and attempts to influence others. Values serve adjustive, ego-defensive, knowledge, and self-actualizing functions. Instrumental and terminal values are related yet are separately organized into relatively enduring hierarchical organizations along a continuum of importance.[11]

Rokeach defined attitudes (that is, persistent tendencies to act in a certain way toward persons, things, situations, or ideas) as a manifestation of values, as follows:

> . . . Values can be conceptualized as the core of cognitive components underlying the thousands of attitudes that people hold, [with] different subsets of values. . . . Whatever the attitude, it is an expression or manifestation of, and should therefore be significantly related to, some subset of terminal and instrumental values.[12]

Rokeach further defined belief as an intention to act, justified by some concept of a desirable mode of behavior of preferred end-state of existence.

The submission of data concerning beliefs, attitudes, and values might seem to give planners a sense of futility in contemplating change were it not for Rokeach's optimistic views concerning the manner in which beliefs are subject to modification. He described his rationale for their modification as follows:

> Such a relative conception of values enables us to define change as a reordering of priorities and, at the same time, to see the total value system as relatively stable over time. It is stable enough to reflect the fact of sameness and continuity of a unique personality socialized within a given culture and society, yet unstable enough to permit rearrangement of value priorities as a result of changes in culture, society, and personal experience.[13]

This conclusion was based on research with McLellan, which had demonstrated that it was possible to modify values, attitudes, and belief. They concluded:

> All that can be concluded thus far on the basis of the existing experimental evidence is that a person's values, attitudes, and behavior will undergo long term changes if objective information about own, and others' value-attitude systems exposes contradictions within one's own value-attitude system to conscious awareness.[14]

It is, then, specifically because values are subject to change that planners are sorely in need of data concerning employees' values, attitudes, and beliefs. And attention in schools must be directed to educational values—what should be done to assist each different kind of student to realize his potential. There is a danger, however, in concentrating exclusively on employees' values; sometimes the institutional value structures make current practices ends unto themselves.

4. Precedents

Employees of institutions often so identify their current values with the operational procedures of the organization that any suggestion for changes in practice produces defensive reactions. Selznick signaled this danger as follows:

> As an organization acquires a self, a distinctive identity, it becomes an institution. This involves taking on of values, ways of acting and believing that are deemed important for their own sake. From then on self-maintenance becomes more than bare organizational survival; it becomes a struggle to preserve the uniqueness of the group in the face of new problems and altered circumstances.[15]

It is, therefore, important for the personnel department to provide planners with information concerning precedents honored and rejected by the employees of the school system.

In this context, there are advantages and disadvantages to a strong degree of institutionalization that must be recognized. On the positive side, it simplifies communication, supports self-maintenance, and facilitates employee cooperation. On the negative side, it promotes limitations of capability to adapt to changing cultural factors, weakens administrative leadership, limits deployment of resources, and diminishes technical and economic justifications for organizational change. It would seem that it is more difficult to bring about change within an institution than in a purely technical organization.

It is, therefore, important that the personnel department provide to planners adequate information concerning employees' self-maintenance behavior. These data should include, minimally, information about employees' attachment to precedent by examining the following behavior:

Resistance to modification of teaching goals, materials, methods.

Reluctance to be transferred to another working group within the organization.

Inability to cooperate with other organizations performing the same or similar services.

Unwillingness to participate in reeducation activities designed to develop new and different skills.

Rejection of new activities or new tasks.

Denial of existence of pressing problems.

Early retirement or resignation following reassignments of duties or work location.

It is clear that this kind of precedent attachment analysis will yield an update on data concerning the extent to which the employee will manifest acceptance of assignments, tasks, relearning, colleagues, and problems. Organizational change is difficult, if not impossible, unless acceptance is forthcoming from a substantial proportion of the workforce.

It is easy to overvalue the defensive reactions of employees who have achieved a high degree of institutional identification; it is seldom absolute. In a complicated, metropolitan society an employee is identified with many social groups. It is, perhaps, important to examine his self-maintenance behavior within other social groups as well as his employment group.

5. *Interaction*

Since employees of school systems are identified with many social groups, it would seem important that planners know the manner in which these different loyalties, activities, and attachments are integrated into work behavior. Sofer has examined the problem as follows:

> The organization member is under its direct influence only part of the day. He has a life apart from the organization, and personal needs and pressures other than those associated with the organization. He has reference groups and membership groups other than those involved on the job. Indeed, part of the contribution of the executive or technical specialist may stem from his external affiliations and identifications, since these help to give him independence of mind and judgment.[16]

Sofer, of course, gave only the most optimistic results from participation in other groups. Other integration patterns may be less productive. Strong identification with other groups may lead to neglect of employment, acceptance of nonproductive work practices, or even disruption of collegial actions. Thus the interaction of an employee with different social groups—and the integration of different loyalties into work behavior—become important to planners in anticipating employees' reactions to changed assignments and responsibilities.

However, the interaction of the employee with different social groups is but one of the interaction problems that need to be documented to planners by the personnel department. The employee interacts with more than one primary group within the organization itself. Sofer stated the problem as follows:

> Organizations consist of overlapping primary groups constituted on the basis of geographic proximity, task similarity, and complementary or linked occupational fate. For the individual organization member, his work life consists of operating memberships of at least one and, more likely, several of these. Since the dominant values of each group differ from each other and from managerial values, there is always some scope for choice by the individual and support in his choices.[17]

In the same sense the employee integrates loyalties, activities, and attachments to different social groups into his work behavior, just so he integrates his loyalties to different primary groups within the organization. Here, pertinent data are most often secured by documenting how he interprets his experiences in one group to the members of other groups with which he is associated.

The problems of securing reliable data concerning the behavior of employees are manifest and their resolution depends, to a large extent, on the energy, leadership, and insight of the personnel administrators. Assuring their use by planners, however, is an organizational question that requires coordinated action of persons occupying many different roles in the resolution of these problems. The extent of the organizational question may be clarified by an examination of planning in school systems.

School System Planning

Planning school systems is done to bring a school, or a school system, in line with current conditions. Plans fall into four main categories:

1. Periodic plans.
2. Long-range plans.
3. Contingency plans.
4. Emergency plans.

Among these, general distinctions are quite clear. Periodic (or recurring) utilization plans may be said to be situational and vary from one administrative unit to another. They are made yearly to maximize goal accomplishment within the constraints of personnel available, support given, and role allocated. Long-range planning, on the other hand, is a never-ending process of developing an image of the organization as it should be at some future time and assessing the organizational changes that are required for its realization. But even long-range planning requires frequent reexamination both of the developing image and its realization through organizational changes. Although Edmund Burke pointed out long ago (1792), "You can never plan the future by the past," the future is uncertain, and is therefore often projected in terms of the past. Long-range plans must be firmly anchored in the events and conditions of the present; while they are being formulated, they require frequent scrutiny and redevelopment. One way of compensating for future uncertainty is to develop alternate plans to adapt to probable, but uncertain, conditions. This is often termed contingency planning and takes into account the need to have plans ready for speedy adaptation to any forseeable set of conditions that may develop. Emergency plans are prepared in times of quiet to cope with problems that may arise in times of stress. The potential of the personnel department to contribute to planning is clarified as each type is examined.

1. Periodic Planning

Periodic utilization plans generally include a host of administrative tasks: determination of vacancies, recruitment, selection, salary determination, assignment, orientation, evaluation, grievances, transfers, termination, retirement, promotion, and skill development.

The personnel administrator is assigned the task of assisting school administrators to develop, assess, revise, and operate plans for the organizational development of each of these administrative acts. Handling this task occupies the major portion of the personnel department's time.

Planning use of behavioral data supplied by the personnel department to predict probable behavior of employees would seem to present a logical and desirable methodology with which to make decisions in these administrative acts. Practice endorses the principle, but behavioral analysis to date has often been rudimentary. In teacher selection, for an example, it has been used by placing undue weight on behavior in practice teaching. In selecting administrators, emphasis has been placed on prior experience as an administrator. This type of behavior analysis is gross, not too predictive of behavior in new situations, and tends to eliminate the consideration of other, more pertinent behavior. If behavioral analysis and prediction are to be used effectively, a greater consensus on purpose and procedures is required.

Productive and incisive planning use of a method such as behavioral analysis cannot be made lightly; it requires careful structuring of a series of planning steps, as follows. The results to be achieved by the organizational unit must be spelled out in terms of the unit's role in the work of the organization as a whole. This means a description not only of the organizational objectives, but also of the role the unit will play in achieving subobjectives. When everyone is aware of the tasks to be completed, the unit must next examine the skills available among the people making up the unit. This activity should then be followed by the assignment of the appropriate individuals to different tasks; this should be done with emphasis on the specific role each is to fulfill, use of the data that give information about employee recorded cooperative interactions with others, and knowledge of the employee's skills in the use of required tools and materials.

This brief description of planning steps serves to underline the planning use of behavioral analysis—to predict with a degree of accuracy whether the work that can reasonably be expected of personnel available will, in fact, accomplish the goals of the unit. For example, if the task of a teacher is to assist each student in a classroom in adopting learning goals for himself, then behavioral analysis would require that performance proof be obtained of his ability to accomplish this objective with each different kind of student in the class.[18] Thus, behavioral analysis presents a means to make assignments to those people who are expected to perform the work intended.

A unit plan for accomplishing objectives, therefore, is dependent upon the performance potential of the individuals assigned to it. Persons assigned may, by joint effort, be able to accomplish all of the objectives fully, partially, or inadequately. Behavioral analysis may direct the administrator in the preparation of other staffing plans. If predictions indicate the unit is overstaffed, excess skills may be made available to other units by personnel transfers. If the staff can be predicted to achieve the necessary skills by short-term, intensive reeducation, it may prompt the creation of an intensive inservice program. If the goals cannot be reached by the predicted efforts of personnel now assigned, it may prompt augmentation by transfers or the employment of other staff members. In all these efforts, the skilled cooperation of the personnel department is vital to goal accomplishment. Nor can it be ignored in long-range planning.

2. Long-Range Planning

The necessity as well as the dangers of long-range planning have long been recognized. The wisdom of the Solomonic proverb, "Where there is no prophecy the people cast off all restraints," is only too apt in some organizations' handling of future planning. School administrators can claim no exception to the truth of this observation. The California Teachers Retirement Fund, for example, has unfunded vested liabilities of at least $5 billion (some estimates have indicated that it may be as much as $9 billion). The ultimate costs of contractual promises made in salary schedules of public school systems—that is, if all teachers worked to retirement age—have been avoided in the past by departures of teachers from the staff prior to retirement. Long-range planning is necessary to avoid untenable futures into which it is possible to blunder.

But it is also possible to construct such a tight long-range plan that paralysis results. For example, Barbara Tuchman referred to the stalemate that came about between the warring principals during World War I. She pointed to the two war plans (that is, German Schlieffen, French No. 17) to which the German and French governments were committed, with neither plan flexible enough to allow adjustment to the military activities of the other.[19]

The greatest danger in long-range planning, however, is not its inflexibility, but its unreality. Since long-range planning requires the development of concepts of alternate futures, the process forever runs the risk of commitments to untenable futures. Most unrealistic futures chosen in long-range planning are untenable because there is no reasonable expectation that the contemplated organization can be staffed with persons possessing the skills, attitudes, and knowledge-uses essential to the completion of the anticipated work. It is, therefore, the personnel department that must provide the data necessary to keep creative speculation within the bounds of reality.

The personnel department, however, is also essential to the development of realistic plans. It is this institutional resource that must assist planners in anticipating (1) skills required of teaching, administrative, and support personnel; (2) assignments of individuals to units and to specific tasks; (3) development of staff potential; (4) morale; and (5) retention.

The first of these may be the most tentative. Indeed, the personnel department may have to use all its resources including intuition, linear projections, analogs, alternative futures, scenarios, and others to be capable of estimating the skills required of the working staff in a selected time target of the future.

Projections of interactions in newly formed working groups may tax the ingenuity of the personnel department as much as projecting the need for skills, but they are equally important to planners. Such projections involve the anticipation of assignments to individuals, the tentative identification of professional consultants, and the clarification of communication patterns within the contemplated work units. This anticipation leads to an examination of the current staff's potential for contributing to different, alternate work groups. It also leads to a consideration of the feasibility of regrouping that may be necessary to reach the contemplated future goals.

An essential part of projecting the probable capacity of contemplated work groups is an assessment of the extent to which inservice education is necessary to maximize their productive potential. If the inservice education requires a period of effort in excess of time constraints placed on the working group by the necessity of goal accomplishment, then the contemplated groups may prove to be impractical. If little or no inservice education is required, it raises the possibility that the contemplated groups are overstaffed. In either event, other groupings of personnel may be indicated.

In addition, the probable effects of the new groupings and modified goals on morale should be considered. If morale is defined as acceptance of goals, confidence in their realization, trust in colleagues, recognized capability of self and others to perform the work, assurance of support within and without the organization for cooperative effort, and recognition of goal accomplishment, then the personnel department can use its recorded data concerning staff values, attitudes, and beliefs to make somewhat tentative projections of morale under the new organization contemplated by planners.

The projections of morale within units and within the school system have the reciprocal effect of identifying those individuals who are most likely to have morale low enough to prompt withdrawal from the changed institution. It will also prompt the consideration of remedial actions that might be taken to challenge attitudes, values, and beliefs with the intent of modifying them to forestall withdrawal.

Thus the engagement of the personnel department in long-range planning may cause the realistic selection of alternate futures and reveal the dimensions of effort required to staff a contemplated changed organization. It may also direct attention to provisional planning to obviate personnel problems likely to result from organizational change.

Some aspects of the selection of alternate futures in long-range planning (often referred to as contingency planning) deserve further analysis.

3. Contingency Planning

Much has been written about the need to provide some shape to the uncertain future. Davis, for an example, pointed out: "Model, schemata, and projection routines provide the planner with methods for fashioning some image of future possibilities in human resource development. Crude routines, they do not shape the future and they may not reveal it very accurately."[20]

Thus prudence dictates the desirability of fashioning alternate images of the future in terms of different, yet reasonable, developmental possibilities. Over time, trends and values will take firmer shape; during frequent reviewing, choices among the images of the future will become more certain and provide a basis for more specific long-range planning. Contingency planning is not a science. It doesn't qualify as an art. But it must become a habit. Without it, personnel administration is a pedestrian process of reacting to demands too late to modify either their insistence, quality, or reasonableness. Without it also the personnel administrator is entangled in a web with harassed administrators, a disappointed staff, critical parents, and frustrated students. This web may become even more frustrating when the emotional pressures of an emergency situation are placed upon the participants.

4. Emergency Planning

Effective adjustment of personnel emergencies depends, to a great extent, upon the degree to which plans made in times of normal operations are known and have anticipated the demands of the emergency. Emergency plans should be made to handle at least the following three situations: (1) unexpected reductions in fiscal support, (2) disasters, and (3) strikes. There are a number of conditions under which these may occur:

Unexpected reductions in fiscal support that result when state or national governments discontinue subsidy or incentive payments.

Taxpayers refuse to pay local taxes or withdraw permission for others to be imposed.

Inflation increases demands for income that taxpayers are unwilling to provide.

State or national regulations place burdens on local taxpayers that they are unwilling to assume.

Fatal accidents occur that remove essential personnel.

Hurricanes, earthquakes, or fires that destroy schools and require reorganization of the working staff.

Employees withdraw services during strikes.

Students refuse to come to school in protest.

Parents withdraw students from school in protest.

Youth gangs disrupt the orderly school operations.

Some of the policies and procedures that should be the topic of emergency planning may be identified by category as follows: staff reduction, transfer, strike, substitutes, student disorders, parent protest, and disasters.

No emergency plan can anticipate with precision the exact nature of the reactions required, but its existence can provide the framework in which more precise actions can be developed.

Summary

An educational institution may be described as "service intensive" in the sense that its goals are achieved through the direct services rendered by its employees. Any planned change is unlikely to be consummated unless the workers accept the tasks willingly, are capable of completing them, and are numerous enough to complete those that are essential. Planning, therefore, requires personnel data most likely to be available to the personnel department.

Essential data should be retrieved for planners from personnel files prepared jointly by the personnel department and the employees. Data may properly include skills, work habits, educational beliefs, precedents accepted and rejected, and interaction patterns in social and primary groups.

Prudence indicates that these data should be sought by administrators in making periodic unit plans, planners in determining the reasonableness of alternate futures, planners in assessing the feasibility of alternate features, and planners in preparing ways of coping with emergencies.

These uses of personnel data in planning requires the personnel department to provide insightful and creative leadership in the recording of personnel data, their retrieval on call, and their use in projecting employee behavior in contemplated changes in work units.

Notes

1. John W. Gardner, *Self Renewal: The Individual and the Innovative Society* (New York: Harper and Row, 1964), chapter 5.
2. Harry S. Broudy, "The Fiduciary Basis of Education: A Crisis in Credibility," *Phi Delta Kappan* 59 (1978):88. ©1978 by Phi Delta Kappa, Inc. Reprinted with permission.
3. Ibid., p. 89. Reprinted with permission.
4. Quoted in V.V.N. Pointer, *History of Education* (New York: D. Appleton and Company, 1886), p. 105.
5. C. Michael Darcy, "Three Stages in the Development of CBTE," *Phi Delta Kappan* 55 (1974):325.
6. Claude W. Fawcett, "The Skills of Teaching," Unpublished mimeographed report to the faculty of the Graduate School of Education, University of California, Los Angeles, May 1965.
7. Robert N. McMurry, *Tested Techniques of Personnel Selection* (Chicago: The Dartnell Corporation, 1966), pp. 4-10.
8. Cyril Sofer, *Organizations in Theory and Practice* (New York: Basic Books, 1972), p. 227.
9. McMurry, *Tested Techniques*, pp. 4-10.
10. William C. Schutz et al., *Procedures for Identifying Persons with Potential for Public School Administrative Positions* (Berkeley: University of California Graduate School of Education, 1961), U.S. Office of Education Cooperative Research Project no. 677, p. 178.
11. Milton J. Rokeach, *The Nature of Human Values* (Glencoe, Ill.: The Free Press, 1973), p. 25.
12. Ibid., p. 95.
13. Ibid., p. 11.

14. Milton J. Rokeach and D. Daniel McLellan, "Feedback of Information about the Attitudes of Self and Others as Determinants of Long Range Cognitive and Behavioral Change," *Journal of Applied Social Psychology* 2 (1972):236-251.

15. Philip Selznick, *Leadership in Administration* (Evanston, Ill.: Row, Peterson, and Company, 1957), p. 21.

16. Sofer, *Organizations*, p. 116.

17. Ibid.

18. C.E. Schneier, "Content Validity: The Necessity of a Behavioral Job Analysis," *Personnel Administrator* 21 (1976):38-44; J.W. Thompson, "Functional Job Descriptions," *Personnel Journal* 30 (1952):380-388.

19. Barbara Tuchman, *The Guns of August* (New York: Macmillan, 1962), pp. 435-440.

20. Russell C. Davis, *Planning Human Resource Development* (Chicago: Rand McNally, 1966), p. 237.

3 Recruitment

In education, the need for constant personnel recruitment is endemic to the profession. A supply of qualified individuals must be maintained to fill educational vacancies as they occur, or can be anticipated. For the past half century, most recruitment procedures developed by school administrators, teacher associations, legislatures, and boards of education have been based on the assumption that administrators, as well as teachers, were interchangeable if they held a license issued by the same state. A scientific administration idea, the concept of intechangeability is a policy based on the idea that efficiency can be standardized and, therefore, duplicated.

Interchangeability, then, continues to guide educational recruitment practices. According to the policy, many educational organizations developed compatible recruitment practices. Teacher associations and teacher-education institutions not only recruited students for license preparation programs, but secondary future teacher organizations were formed to foster high-school students' interests in the profession. State departments of education, acting according to the policy, formulated license requirements in terms of courses to be completed. State approval went easily to institutions willing to offer the state pattern of courses. Approved institutions were allowed to designate graduates to receive licenses. Accepting the policy, certification was required by boards of education; and, in periods of teacher shortages, temporary licenses were sought by them for thousands of individuals, thus maintaining the policy while compromising its intent.

Recent developments in state licensing have not seriously modified the policy of interchangeability. The Competency- (Perfomance-) Based Teacher Licensing systems, initiated in 1974, merely required institutions to prove how required courses developed competencies. By 1973, seventeen states had modified their licensing laws to embrace some form of competency-based licensing.[1] Tennessee mandated the program for administrators only. As early as 1974 Rosner and Kay had identified the difficulties inherent in the competency-based system. They suggested that "competency-based teacher education has come to mean so many things to so many people, the real promise is unlikely to be realized," adding as a prediction that "it will be washed away, ironically, by currents of ambiguity."[2]

Their prediction was soon confirmed. In 1976, Roth investigated 215 institutions reported to have CBTE programs. Evaluating data received from sixty of these, he concluded that "a major problem with the information reported on competency-based teacher education is that CBTE is not the same from institution to institution."[3]

Such results suggest that the CBTE attempt to relate licensing practices to specific teaching acts did not really come to grips with the issues that eluded all previous licensing systems as well: a lack of consensus regarding (1) the goals of education and (2) appropriate professional behavior. And it is the growing diversity of these two issues in large, metropolitan school districts which may be making state licensing systems obsolete.

The diversity of school populations has grown with metropolitanization. Schools have attempted to take on a larger share of the entire community educational program. In doing so, schools, according to Goodlad, "like some self-destructive dinosaur, seek to adapt by growing larger." He continued: ". . . The more they take on, the fewer resources they have for and the less attention they give to their education function. Ironically, the more they take on, the less other institutions assume responsibility for education." Nor is he hopeful about the development of adequate educational procedures. He pointed out: "We are a badly divided profession, with each segment perceiving only a part of the whole, lacking awareness of and commitment to the systematic, collaborative functioning required for significant improvement.

Goodlad recommended decentralization of goals and the development of procedures to each school unit, as follows: ". . . Schools will be better if legislators, school board members, parents, and superintendents see themselves as responsible and accountable for enhancing the effectiveness, unity, and sense of mission of the single school."[4]

If this presents an acceptable solution to coping with metropolitan educational needs, the justification of state-mandated curricula, accountability systems that include minimum competency regulations and complex state licenses, and school assumption of the educational activities of other institutions becomes more and more difficult. Furthermore, the concept of interchangeability of licensees appears less and less tenable.

However, the human relations approach to personnel recruitment cannot offer a much more effective program. Elevating group compatibility to the position of prime consideration in recruitment forced the derogation of criteria of skill and knowledge to positions of lesser importance during the human relations period (circa 1930-1957). Yet skill and knowledge are crucial to the goal accomplishment of social systems administration.

Planning for Recruitment

If skill and knowledge, instead of group compatibility, are to be prime criteria in recruitment, the personnel department is required to work cooperatively with unit administrators in

1. Auditing unit personnel tasks and skills.
2. Maximizing the use of personnel resources.
3. Determining the needs for additional personnel.

1. Auditing Unit Personnel Tasks and Skills

Tasks. A unit task audit requires (1) that the tasks be confirmed by the role assigned and (2) that they be authenticated by the educational needs of the student body. The tasks a single school is expected to complete are defined by the role assigned to it in the school system. The role is established to assure unified effort among schools of the system and coordination with nonschool community educational institutions. But teachers, like employees of all other organizations, tend to give more time to the work they do best, or for which they receive the most approbation. Periodic auditing of tasks selected by teachers, and their confirmation or disqualification by referral to the unit's role, can assure the following in planning for recruitment.

> The maintenance of a dynamic and current role definition for the school.
>
> The development and maintenance of a viable set of tasks to be accepted and completed by the school.
>
> Redirection of personnel whose choices of tasks, either because of personal preference or skills, have led to the acceptance of tasks assigned to colleagues, other institutions, or other schools in the system.

But the tasks confirmed by the school's role may need to be amended by an audit of the learning needs of the students in the school. Children and youth of the same age differ so much in abilities, interests, and achievement that it is unthinkable that they should be presented with the same learning fare and be expected to make the same progress. A unit task audit should, therefore, confirm the status of the desired skills, attitudes, and knowledge uses in the student body. Using these data, the staff should professionally designate the most appropriate learning sequences for each different kind of student. As students for whom the same or similar learning sequences are appropriate are grouped together for instruction, the general teaching tasks defined by the unit's role are made specific. Task descriptions can then be used to identify the full range of teaching skills required for their completion. They can be classified as (1) minimum for task acceptance, (2) required for continuation in the assignment, (3) desirable for all experienced teachers, (4) outstanding for professional leadership, and (5) exceptional for inservice development of others. Thus the task audit carries the planning burden of task identification and explication so that the determination of unit capability can be examined first by an audit of skills possessed by the current staff.

Skills. Teaching skills can be classified as classroom management, use of professional knowledge, and interaction with students and colleagues. The classroom management skills may be identified as follows:

Capability for helping each kind of student in the unit to develop learning goals for himself;

Helping each kind of student to utilize the most effective learning procedures to reach his goals;

Success in reinforcing each kind of desirable student learning behavior, redirecting undesirable behavior, and developing confident self-evaluation techniques;

Facility in developing student decision-making skills about learning activities;

Helping students to examine objectively evidence about problems, even evidence repugnant to them;

Ability to assist students in monitoring their own development by keeping records of skills attained, attitudes modified, and characteristic uses of knowledge;

Facility in assisting each kind of student to integrate school and nonschool learning activities;

Capability for helping students to develop skills in communicating with fellow students, staff members, parents, the public, and nonschool educational leaders;

Helping each kind of student to make maximum use of the class in reaching his learning goals; and

Assisting each kind of student to establish priorities in his learning activities.

Skills in the use of professional knowledge may be identified as follows:

Sequencing instruction for the development of cognitive, affective, and skill learned by each kind of student in the unit;

Helping each kind of student in the unit to make discriminating use of the available tools and materials of instruction;

Diagnosis of learning difficulties encountered by each kind of student in the unit; and

Capacity for creating a challenging learning environment for each kind of student in the unit.[5]

Skills required for interacting with students and colleagues should be examined within the framework of "motivational behavior" of individuals within the working group. McMurry suggested the following list of behaviors as significant and recurring:

Self-aggrandizement;

Security;

Approval;

Authority;

Curiosity;

Competitiveness;

Perfectionism; and

Desire for service.[6]

An audit of the skills possessed by the current staff, when compared with the skills required to complete the tasks assigned to the school, can produce a preliminary estimate of tasks that can be accepted. But that preliminary estimate may be amended by the adoption of procedures to maximize the use of skills available.

2. *Maximizing the Use of Personnel Resources*

There are many instances in which a skills inventory will disclose that essential skills are concentrated in a few members of the staff. When this is discovered, two alternatives seem most appropriate: (1) an organizational arrangement can be adopted that fosters short-time exposure of many students to the skilled teacher, or (2) a skill transfer system can be developed.

If the administrator opts for the first alternative of short-time exposure to a skilled teacher by many students, several courses of action are open. Responsive to such a choice, Goodlad and Anderson suggested the ungraded school.[7] Stoddard suggested a semidepartmental procedure called "The Dual Progress Plan."[8] This plan employs a graded system with a part of the curriculum and an ungraded system with the rest, with specialist teachers recommended for both. But because the adoption of either of these plans has often been difficult, if not impossible, in a climate of building limitations, scarcity of instructional materials, and frequent public opposition to change (read, nostalgia for the "basics"), many administrators have chosen the second alternative of skill transfer.

Skill transfer techniques have included supervision, workshops, action research, classroom visitation, inservice collegiate courses, coaching, and reading-study programs. Dempsey and Smith endorsed a highly organized skill transfer system named "Differentiated Staffing."[9] All of these have been used and are acceptable if the skill shortages are judged to be correctable with relatively brief instruction. However, too much reliance on their efficacy may produce instances of unrealistic employment and assignment of inexperienced personnel. If the skill requirements of the unit staff are greater than can be corrected by these two devices for maximizing skills available, it is necessary to tread a more difficult path and consider transfers, terminations, or employment of additional personnel.

3. Determining the Needs for Additional Personnel

This planning process should facilitate the recruiting activities of the personnel department by providing the following information about each vacancy to be filled:

The tasks to be assigned.

Maximum desirable skills to be displayed in the assignment.

Minimum skills acceptable for beginning the assignment.

Time constraints for developing skills not possessed at the time of appointment.

Interaction skills needed for student leadership and collegial cooperation.

Uses of knowledge required in the assignment.

It is only at this point, with the planning complete and the data it produces at hand, that the personnel department can be considered ready to turn to the sources of supply where qualified individuals may be found. They are found in three main markets: (1) a general, national market; (2) the organization itself; and (3) other educational employers.

The General Market

A high rate of transiency in the teaching profession, not only in and out of school districts, but in and out of the profession, requires emphasis on a general, national market for securing adequate educational personnel. Transiency is pointed up by a recent study conducted by the National Education Association. It reported that in the 1975-76 school year nearly a third (32.3 percent) of all teachers had five or fewer years of experience; only one in six (16.9 percent) had twenty or more years; over half (65.4 percent) had four or less years of experience in the school district in which they were employed in 1975-76.[10] This rate of transiency translates into the replacement of one in ten teachers, principals, and supervisors each year in a total national staff of approximately 2.4 million.[11] Only judicious use of all sources of supply in the general market is likely to provide personnel of the quality and quantity needed.

The sources of supply in the general market are:

Placement offices of teacher preparing institutions, private employment advisers, teacher associations, state employment services, and administrator organizations.

Advertisements.

Voluntary applications.

Members of the profession.

The development of these sources of supply becomes an obligation of the personnel department. One of the most important is placement offices.

Placement Offices

It is important to develop placement officers as partners in search for needed personnel. In developing the partnership, information should be provided that includes the characteristics of the community, its educational program, the role of the school in the community, the district's record as an employer, and its accomplishments as an educational institution. This information is found in district policy manuals, reports, community surveys, economic reports, census data, and public relations documents. Any or all of these should be disseminated to placement officers. They present general district data and provide a contextual framework for requisitions when they are presented. Requisitions add further meaning by supplying precise information about each vacancy listed. Requisitions should generally include such items as (1) tasks to be assigned, that is, level of skill required for appointment, eventual level desired, and time constraints for full skill development, and (2) specifications of interaction skills required to foster staff cooperation and student leadership. The record of acceptance and rejection of candidates recommended to the district should be kept up to date and provided to placement officers. This assists them in understanding the intent of the district in the use of their services. It is self-evident that this information flow to placement officers can only prove effective if the district maintains a constant information exchange with them by frequent visits of recruiting personnel or telephone conversations. But this close working relationship with placement offices may need to be supplemented by development of other sources of supply. Advertising has a limited but important role in recruiting.

Advertisements

Newspaper or journal announcements and publications prepared by districts are most useful to satisfy affirmative action requirements for the notification of vacancies to all qualified persons in the recruiting area. Efficiency suggests that the content of the announcements provide adequate data for a process of self-screening. Essential data for that purpose are the same as information listed in requisitions submitted to placement offices, including interaction skills required for group participation and expected uses of knowledge. The reader of the announcement should have sufficient information to decide whether (1) the position is one of high or low risk for his stage of professional development, (2) the group is one in which he can work successfully, and (3) his knowledge base is adequate to accept the tasks to be assigned. Neither the skill of writing such an announcement nor the selection of publication sources has, to date, reached a high level of effectiveness, but specifying the goals in this type of recruitment is essential. Self-selection, however, is not new to educational recruitment—it has, heretofore, taken the form of voluntary application.

Voluntary Application

There are many reasons, transcending the work per se, which account for individuals offering their services to specific educational institutions. For example, community amenities: beach cities are more attractive to some than inland towns; ski areas are attractive to others; fishing opportunities appeal to some; the proximity of a school district to a graduate school is desirable to the ambitious scholar; metropolitan areas are often culturally attractive; or a district's reputation—deserved or not—is often a motivating factor. The list is almost as endless as the variety of ways people are motivated, but whatever the attraction is based upon, the personnel department should treat these applicants as a valuable resource because a voluntary choice of district by the employee diminishes the employer's problem of motivating personnel. This source of supply is handled by prompt acknowledgment of the application, full response concerning current vacancies, and periodic renewal of applications kept on file. However, caution must be exercised in using this source of supply: too great a reliance on voluntary applications may cost other opportunities to improve the quality of the staff. There are many persons, with scarce and desired skills, who are not actually looking for employment. Sometimes these can be found only with the cooperation of other members of the profession.

Members of the Profession

The development of members of the profession as a source of supply is based on the mutual needs of employers and employees. For example, it may be that the current employer is unable to utilize the scarce skills that the employee possesses; or a management development program has produced more administrators than can be used; or the individual recommended has changed his residence and another employer would simplify a commuting problem; or a spouse has changed employment and a change of residence would be more convenient. This resource development requires regular information exchanges between the personnel department and professors in teacher education institutions, other personnel administrators, and administrators who supervise inservice development programs. As in the case of all recruitment, the information should include precise information concerning the assignment, the community, and the district, thereby enabling members of the profession to make recommendations with confidence. This source of supply, however, should stand the cost-benefit test applied to all sources.

Evaluation of Sources of Supply

Probably the ultimate test of adequacy of sources of supply may well be the number of applications received from individuals who are qualified for the vacancies that have been published. The number, undoubtedly, will vary according to the type of assignment. McMurry computed some of these variables and found that an insurance firm needed five applicants to employ an office worker; an industrial firm needed ten to employ a machinist; and some organizations required forty to fifty applicants to employ an executive.[12] Numbers of applicants—some qualified but most unqualified—rise when advertising is used as a source. The district experience can, and should, provide, if records are kept accurately, standards for determining the number of applicants needed for each type of assignment. Cost factors dictate that sources of supply which provide large numbers of unqualified applicants, or few applicants, should be eliminated, while other sources should be added until the district receives an adequate number of qualified applicants.

Another test of the adequacy of sources of supply is the extent to which applicants reflect the various subcultures of the community. A school system, because it includes children and youth, requires a staff of teachers who understand all subcultures well enough to respond pedagogically to each student. The interactions of staff members from different cultures facilitate staff adaptation to, and mastery of, the appropriate responses. Before affirmative action legislation was enacted in the mid-1960s, this concept of staff differentiation was generally expressed as a balance in ages, sexes, skills, and sometimes skin color. Legislation has changed the definition of balance to mean representation of all subcultures on the staff. Laws and regulations spell out procedures for securing this kind of balance, thus adding a new dimension to the development of adequate sources of supply.

Affirmative Action: Legal Bases and a Four-Step Model

Federal laws mandating affirmative action do not normally apply to local school districts, but they have often been imposed—in part or in whole—as a condition for receiving federal subsidies. However, state laws and local regulations adopted under political pressures from constituencies have frequently sought credibility by being modeled after the federal regulations. The most pertinent federal standards are provided by Title VII of the Civil Rights Act of 1964, as amended by the Equal Opportunity Act of 1972; Presidential Executive Orders 11246, 11375, 11141, 11478, 11758; the Equal Pay Act of 1963 as amended by the Education Amendments of 1972; the Age Discrimination Act of 1967; and the National Labor Relations Act of 1947, as amended by the Labor Management Reporting Act of 1959.[13] Because it is reasonable to expect more school districts and states to adopt similar laws and regulations, an examination of the federal model for affirmative action may clarify the problem for school district recruiting. The model includes four steps.

Affirmative Action Model

> Identification of affirmative action units in which balance is to be maintained;
>
> Audits of units for balance in race, color, age, sex, religion, and national origin;
>
> Determination of the availability of personnel with these characteristics, who are qualified for the positions available, and who want to use them in the district, in the normal district recruiting areas; and
>
> Amendment of imbalance by using vacancies created by retirements, resignations, and terminations.[14]

Affirmative Action Units

In public schools, affirmative action units in which balance is to be achieved may be interpreted to include each building work group, each support department or group of departments with comparable work assignments, and, because of the possibility of sex discrimination, the trainees in the administrative development program. In colleges and universities such units may mean each major department, school, support department, or group of departments.

Once a unit has been designated, an affirmative action officer should be selected. In public schools, this might typically be the building principal; in a single support department, the department head; in a group of departments, one of the department heads. The intent of the law is not merely to designate a unit, but to appoint an individual to be responsible for securing and maintaining balance in the staff.

Audits

It is the affirmative action officer's responsibility to determine the extent to which the current staff fairly represents the subcultures of the community. This is not an easy task because the data required to make such determinations have often been excluded from personnel files to prevent discriminating in hiring. Surely, surnames are not infallible as indicators of ethnicity. And age distributions, which require examination of retirement records, require multiple calculations. The audit of staff distribution may, therefore, be an approximation, the accuracy of which depends on the acceptance of, and trust in, the intentions of the affirmative action officer.

He can, however, be more confident of the composition of the community and its subcultures by use of census data provided to him by the personnel department. Census data, though traditionally somewhat inaccurate, are acceptable indicators to most persons interested in affirmative action. But plans to correct imbalances discovered in audits do not always reach quick fruition; delays may be caused by such matters as the availability of qualified minority personnel.

Determination of Personnel Availability

The incorporation of affirmative action requirements into recruiting calls for the accurate delineation by the personnel department of the market area from which each different kind of employee is secured. The areas may be quite limited for certain categories of personnel. A carpenter, for example, living on the east side of a large metropolitan area may be unwilling to be considered for a position on the west side. A secretary may not be able to afford more than a ten-mile commuting distance to work. A teacher may be unwilling to travel more than a few miles because of family responsibilities. Restrictions on travel, therefore, may reduce the area of search for any class of employee. Recruiting area limits can be determined from the personnel experience of the district, such as reasons for terminations or resignations, and records of personnel performance. Specificity is all important, because the personnel department must follow the geographical determinations with an intensive survey of each area to determine the extent of availability of personnel with different characteristics who are qualified for, and seek, service in the district.

Amendment of Imbalance

A concluding step in affirmative recruiting is the development of long-range plans for correcting imbalance. This planning is done jointly by the personnel department, administrators, and the various unit affirmative action officers. Data required for such planning are:

Relation of the composition of the unit workforce to the community subcultures.

Availability of qualified candidates with different subculture characteristics in the community.

Opportunities to modify staff composition provided by expected retirements, terminations, and resignations.

Using these data, a plan may be prepared to provide successive yearly recruitment targets required to correct imbalances. Even though projections are generally made five years in advance, planning should be done each year to allow for changes in candidate availability and staff composition.

The use of affirmative action criteria—along with cost-benefit standards—to evaluate sources of supply is intended to facilitate their modification until they supply adequate numbers of candidates for each vacancy. But numbers are not adequate until they make it possible for a unit administrator to choose—among several alternatives—a preferred staff organization to get work done. Adequate numbers may then be defined as sufficient when the group of applicants contains qualified persons capable of staffing any contingent organizational plan perceived as tenable in the planning process. Recruitment screening is designed to identify candidates capable of providing this freedom of choice.

Recruitment Screening

This type of recruitment screening requires sophisticated use of (1) applications; (2) the personal interview; and (3) in some cases, medical screening.

Applications

The screening potential of applications has often been lost because personnel administrators, or screening committees, have substituted personal experience, organizational stereotypes, or intuition—for district experience—as criteria for evaluating data. A concern for equity suggests that district experience be used in establishing criteria. This concept, although not yet generally used, is referred to as the "Weighted Application."[15] It works as follows.

The procedure asks for weights (usually 0-5 in increasing value) to be assigned after the analysis of the district's experience with each different employee who answered the question differently. If, for an example, the district has lost most inexperienced female college graduates within three years of original employment, and before reaching maximum professional competence, then that response should be rated 0, 1, or 2 on the weighted application. If, on the other hand, an experienced female teacher returning to teaching after a seven-year break for family responsibilities has tended to render good service until retirement, then that response should be rated 3, 4, or 5 on the application. If spouses of sales people tend to remain in the district for no more than two to five years because of transiency in that occupation, that factor should be rated 0, 1, or 2. If, on the other hand, the spouse is engaged in a privately owned business and the employee has tended to be permanent in the district, the weighting should be 3, 4, or 5. The criteria for deciding values of application responses are thus drawn from the experience of the district.

Other common application responses that can be weighted according to district experience are the following:

Frequency of changes of address.

Number of spouses (revealed only for a female applicant when all names under which records and work history have been accumulated).

Educational history (divided for weighting into segments pertinent to practice of skills that have been identified as significant).

Noneducational work history (divided into segments pertinent to the practice of skills that have been identified as significant).

Special activities (for example, an athlete still competing, refereeing, or coaching; service in the military reserves; thespian activities; writing; or supplementary occupations).

Uses of tools and materials of instruction (for example, computer expertise, software construction, film production and editing, text writing, materials construction, evaluation expertise).

Medical history.

Salary or income preferences.

Ages of children and youth dependents.

After weighting of these factors in terms of values derived from district experience, a choice can be made of the highest scoring applicants to be subjected to further screening. The number selected is a function of the contingency plans made during work anticipation. It is common to follow application screening with a personal interview.

Personal Interviews

The screening interview provides data that cannot be secured from the application (for example, elaboration of application responses that are obscure, incomplete, or persented in a manner calculated to obfuscate). It provides an opportunity for sight screening of physical impairment, manner of dress, and relaxation under stress. It creates opportunities for face-to-face evaluation of speech, diction, visual acuity, and alacrity of interview responses. But the interview must be conducted with skill and care; discretion must be used in problematic areas. For example, the interview should not be used to infer character from appearance even though there is a tendency for interviewers to do this in the first five minutes of an interview—termed "gating"—and then spend the rest of the time trying to justify the snap evaluation.[16] A conscious rejection of this tendency can be facilitated by concentration on the purposes mentioned above. In addition, caution in the use of sight data is indicated. None of them, taken singly, should disqualify a candidate, nor should any be reported to the candidate as reason for failure to consider the application further. They can be considered, along with all other data, in forming a prediction of the risk to the candidate and the district of employment.

Medical Screening

Even though medical screening (for example, chest x-rays to determine the presence of tuberculosis) may be required of finalists in the selection process to determine the presence of a communicable disease, it is seldom appropriate in recruitment. It is sometimes done at the request of a candidate whose medical profile shows a history of physical impairment to demonstrate current capacity for the tasks to be assigned. If such a request is made, the district and the candidate may properly share the expense. Each gains by the procedure: the candidate is reassured of physical competence, and the district gains useful data for the recruiting process of selecting qualified individuals most likely to complete the assigned tasks.

The culmination of recruitment screening is the selection of a group of applicants with diverse enough skills to provide the unit administrator freedom of choice in staff organization. The group should be composed of individuals most likely to be able to accept the assigned tasks, complete them, and remain in the organization long enough to justify the cost of selection.

This last consideration is important because the use of the general market is costly, as it was before the intensive recruitment activities required by affirmative action. Also, the development of sources of supply, their continuous evaluation, and the screening of applicants is time-consuming. But more is involved than reduction of costs in making full use of organizational recruiting (employee transfers) in recruiting for vacancies.

The Organization as a Market: Transfers

Employee transfers are essential for staff motivation as well as to find the right person for a vacancy. In a school system, as in most working situations, little remains constant, least of all the employees who are responsible for keeping the system going. They develop new skills; or they lose or modify skills already possessed because of illness, accident, or age; or they become bored with repetitive work; or they are ambitious and seek advancement; or they display a combination of several of these factors. Personal life arrangements, away from the employing organization, may change income, housing, and professional needs. Further, tenured personnel—as much as others—need to know that job enrichment, enlargement, or redesign are available to them.[17] Such assurance may not only lead them to more rewarding activities; it may stimulate and otherwise motivate them to break out of routines. But motivation is only one justification for recruiting among persons already employed. Another important consideration is cost.

Screening and selection costs can be reduced by employee transfers. Orientation may be less extensive, and thus less expensive. The probability of error in selection may be reduced, because the employee has in the records of the personnel department a documented work and skill history. Screening is simplified because the data are available in the files. But desirable though such cost-effectiveness is, transfers become onerous when they are forced by staff reductions resulting from, say declining, enrollments.

In school districts—as in government, business, industry, and other private organizations—the common policy is to meet staff reductions by seniority layoffs, last in/first out procedures. This practice is often required by collective bargaining agreements. But seniority agreements, however viable, ignore skill criteria; thus it is important that the most advantageous reallocations of those left be made. A reasonable concern for goal accomplishment suggests that staff planning and recruitment procedures be used to reorganize the continuing staff. If this is to be done, the transfer policies should incorporate the following decisions: (1) the use of a staff skill inventory procedure, (2) staff searches for recruitment of appropriate personnel, and (3) declaration of the intent of transfers in the organization according to established transfer policies.

Skill Inventories

A record of each employee's skills may be kept as an adjunct to the payroll record. Data storage can be a relatively simple process when computer space is readily available. They can be kept current by the incorporation of findings from evaluations, unit audits, and inservice education programs. They are, of course, useful when they indicate capabilities for performing essential educational services. They are similarly useful when skills are diminished by illness, accident, age, or lack of practice, because they facilitate transfer to less demanding assignments. And the data bank is indispensable in searching for personnel to fill vacancies.

Staff Searches

A reasonable concern both for economy and the motivation of personnel would seem to suggest that employees should have first claim on assignments in the district. If they are to be provided this opportunity, the first recruiting step would be a search of records to identify working individuals qualified to fill identified vacancies. After identification, the personnel department would do well to give those employees an opportunity for first refusal. It must be pointed out that such positive recruitment of currently employed personnel is at variance with present practices of posting vacancies to urge voluntary application. But even if other reasons (for example, employment contracts) dictate a continuation of posting, the first selection act after notification would also have to be a search of records to verify competence for the vacancy. This kind of positive program for maximizing the use of staff skills may, however, run aground on employee resistance if the intent and procedures of transfer have not been developed with the staff.

Transfer Policies

There are a number of policies the staff should consider and assist in developing. Transfer policies should consider the following:

Balance the subculture representation in work units.

Provide opportunities for employees to work at their highest skill level.

Use all staff skills maximally for the completion of educational goals.

Accommodate personnel to compensate for illnesses, physical impairment, or diminished physical resources.

Fulfill employees' developing interests.

Facilitate teachers' transfers to administration.

Enable employees to join more compatible work groups.

Facilitate transfers to positions in more compatible community settings.

Staff participation in the determination of transfer policies may reveal some policy concerns regarding

Opportunities to refuse proposed reassignments.

Organizational restrictions on commuting distances in making reassignments.

Timespan of service required in reassigned position.

Fiscal incentives provided to encourage acceptance of new assignments.

But even the most effective use of personnel available in the system does not add individuals needed to fill vacancies created by terminations, resignations, retirements, and expanded services. Although new personnel can probably be secured in the general market, it is often profitable, in terms of both time and money, to recruit first among cooperative educational employers in the same metropolitan area.

Other Organizations as a Market: Cooperation among Districts

Cooperative exchanges of personnel between different school districts in the same metropolitan area would seem to create a larger, more diverse talent pool likely to be beneficial to all participants. But there are practices, hardened over the years into quasi-traditions, that present barriers to such a course of action. These are

Tenure restricted to the district of employment.

Higher salaries paid in some suburban districts.

Reluctance of some teachers to work in the inner city.

Travel distances for commuting in metropolitan school districts.

District reputations—deserved or not.

If these barriers can be removed in part, or in whole, recruiting benefits gained may be (1) cooperative recruitment, and (2) exchanges of personnel.

Cooperative Recruitment

Recruiting in one district may identify individuals—if needs of other districts are known—who could be used by other employers. A reasonable concern for economy would seem to prompt cooperation of districts in the same metropolitan area. This cooperation could logically be extended to the joint consideration of surplus personnel, whether made surplus by reductions in staff, an oversupply of administrative personnel, or underuse of talent in the employing district. And these exchanges of recruitment information may well lead to exchanges of personnel.

Exchanges of Personnel

Exchanges of personnel between districts in metropolitan areas may be of a permanent or a temporary nature. Permanent exchanges are likely to be the product of the employment of surplus personnel by another district. Such exchanges now take place within the general market procedure and consist of the surplus employee's entering the market and finding employment wherever there is a vacancy. The result of this may be less than desirable, particularly if it means losing a person who could provide his greatest service in the metropolitan area in which he has had experience. It would seem that metropolitan districts would be well advised to retain an experienced metropolitan teacher within its confines. But exchanges of personnel on a temporary basis may be beneficial without such drawbacks.

There are various occasions that require temporary exchanges. Occasionally a district needs skilled leadership for a particular activity only for the period necessary to develop its own personnel. Or a district may have the luxury of a surplus employee whose services will be needed at a future date. A loan arrangement that will enable a district to retain the employment rights of the individual being loaned can be worked out. Loans may be used, furthermore, to provide intern experiences for individuals who need to gain work experiences in (1) subcultures not represented in the employing district, (2) organizations using different administrative or organizational policies, or (3) schools using different instructional procedures.

Although cooperative recruiting and exchanges of personnel may not satisfy more than a few of a district's personnel needs, cooperation on these matters may serve to diminish the competition for personnel now characteristic of most metropolitan areas.

Summary

Recruitment provides a supply of individuals to fill educational vacancies as they occur or can be anticipated. Vacancies are determined by a joint planning process conducted by the personnel department and unit administrators that includes (1) a unit audit of tasks and staff skills to complete them, (2) choices of alternatives to maximize the use of skills available, and (3) the determination of the skills needed by recruits. Three recruiting arenas may be developed by the personnel department: a general market, transfers within the organization, and other educational employers.

Full development of the general market requires skillful cooperation with placement officers, judicious use of advertising, grateful acceptance of voluntary applications, and collegial cooperation with other members of the profession. Sources of supply should stand the tests of cost-benefit and the provision of an adequate supply of affirmative action candidates. Sources that fail these tests should be eliminated. Others should be added until an adequate supply of candidates is available.

Screening of candidates from general market sources may be done by using applications, interviews, and sometimes medical screening. Only candidates most likely to succeed in the district—determined by district personnel experience—should be recommended for the fine screening of selection. But, whenever possible, the group recommended for final selection should display skills diverse enough to allow a unit administrator freedom of choice in using any staff organization identified as feasible in the planning process. And the general market should not be used exclusively; transfers within the organization also serve other important organizational purposes.

Transfers of personnel within the organization can be used to combat boredom, maximize the use of skills, adjust to diminish employee capacities, give evidence of advancement, select teachers for administrative posts, and reorganize the staff during periods of staff reduction. Transfer effectiveness may be enhanced by the maintenance of skill inventories, frequent staff searches, and the development of an equitable transfer policy. However, transfers do not add to the staff; general market recruiting does, but it is expensive. A less expensive method may be developed by recruiting in other school districts.

Recruiting in other school districts may reduce the hazards of intense competition—salary bidding, restricted tenure, and district ballyhoo—if attention is directed to cooperative recruiting, sharing of surplus personnel, loans of individuals with unique skills, and joint conduct of inservice development programs. But, useful though these cooperative techniques may be, most of the recruiting of additional personnel will have to be done in the general market.

Notes

1. Alfred P. Wilson and William W. Curtis, "The States Mandate Performance Based Teacher Education," *Phi Delta Kappan* 55 (1973):76-77.

2. Benjamin Rosner and Patricia M. Kay, "Will the Promise of CBTE Be Fulfilled?" *Phi Delta Kappan* 55 (1974):290-295.

3. Robert A. Roth, "How Effective Are CBTE Programs?" *Phi Delta Kappan* 58 (1977):757-760.

4. John I. Goodlad, "Can Our Schools Get Better?" *Phi Delta Kappan* 60 (1979):342-347.

5. Claude W. Fawcett, "The Skills of Teaching," Unpublished mimeographed report to the faculty of the Graduate School of Education, University of California, Los Angeles, May 1965.

6. Robert N. McMurry, *Tested Techniques of Personnel Selection* (Chicago: The Dartnell Corporation, 1966), section 7, pp. 6-11.

7. John I. Goodlad and Robert H. Anderson, *The Nongraded Elementary School* (New York: Harcourt, Brace, and World, 1963).

8. George D. Stoddard, *The Dual Progress Plan* (New York: Harper and Row, 1961).

9. Richard A. Dempsey and Rodney F. Smith, Jr., *Differentiated Staffing* (Englewood Cliffs, N.J.: Prentice-Hall, 1972).

10. National Education Association, *Status of the American Public School Teacher: 1975-1976* (Washington, D.C.: The Association, 1977), p. 15.

11. U.S. Bureau of the Census, *Statistical Abstract of the United States: 1976* (Washington, D.C.: U.S. Government Printing Office, 1976), p. 129.

12. McMurry, *Personnel Selection*, section 2, p. 13.

13. James M. Higgins, "A Manager's Guide to the Equal Employment Opportunity Laws," *Personnel Journal* 55 (1976):406-411.

14. J. Stanley Pottinger, "Administering a Solution, Goals vs. Quotas," *Journal of the College and University Personnel Association* 26 (1975):21-25. Used with permission of the *Journal of the College and University Personnel Association.*

15. G.W. England, Development and Use of Weighted Application Blanks (Minneapolis: University of Minnesota Industrial Relations Center, 1971).

16. E.C. Webster, *Decision Making in the Employment Interview* (Montreal: McGill University Industrial Relations Center, 1964).

17. J.R. Maher, *New Prescriptions in Job Enrichment* (New York: D. Van Nostrand, 1971).

4 Fine Screening: The Selection Process

Fine screening of candidates is a process designed to provide unit administrators an opportunity to select a qualified individual for the staffing of one of the unit's alternative work plans. The process in social systems administration differs from the scientific administration approach, in which confirmation of licensed capabilities is reviewed by examining practice teaching reports, determination of the extent of the candidate's knowledge by reliance on grade point averages and courses taken, and typical behavior established by examining reports submitted as recommendations by friends and former teachers. It also differs from the human relations approach, in which compatible group members are selected often by committee action. Both scientific and human relations administrators use final selection to secure one candidate to fill a prescribed vacancy. The social systems procedure, on the other hand, is designed to provide personnel options enabling the administrator to choose, among alternatives, the most feasible work plan. Decisions about feasibility are mere speculation unless the expected work behavior of each candidate is estimated in fine screening. The personnel department makes this possible, to the degree evidence is available, by undertaking the following:

Validating applicants' records.

Confirming the possession of skills.

Analyzing work habits.

Securing candidates' reactions to prior assignments.

The validation of records is an essential first step—the other steps may not be taken if records prove to be inaccurate.

Validation of Records

It is to be expected, in view of the vagaries of human nature, that application data supplied by candidates are not always accurate. Almost every personnel office is the repository of at least one horror story of counterfeited transcripts, falsified licenses, or distorted work histories.

Some have discovered inaccurate reports of prior accomplishments, honors, or recognition. Some have discovered inaccuracies caused by haste, self-congratulatory distortion, faulty memory, or self-delusion. Although a measure of validation assistance can be given by reputable placement offices, their efforts usually are concentrated on three concerns: (1) authenticity of licenses, (2) accuracy of employment dates, and (3) reasons for changing positions. Other placement offices, less well supported and pushed for time, often are able to provide only a listing of services each candidate can render and recommendations written by former teachers and employers. But there are a number of ways confidence in candidates' statements can be assured; notably, by consultation with colleges and universities, with former supervisors, and with each successive employer. To accomplish some or all of these types of consultation, McMurry recommended the use of the "telephone check."[1]

The Telephone Check

One of the advantages of the telephone check is that it may be more prompt, as well as less expensive, than mail or personal visitation. Its usefulness, however, can be impaired if the questions to be asked are not properly planned. Indeed, a form should be designed for this purpose, including printed questions to be asked and space for appropriate entries for the responses to be received. For many types of positions, such a form can be standardized because the same questions are repetitive. In cases in which assignments are unique, separate forms should be prepared.

Each organization normally employs some persons able to provide validation data; experience will assist the personnel officer in identifying them. Rarely, and then only with the candidate's written permission, should a current employer be queried. In most cases, the personnel department of the former employer will be able to supply data from the records; sometimes, when it does not have the data, it may have to identify supervisors from whom information is to be secured. The telephone may also be used in checking on the accuracy of scholastic records.

Scholastic Records

Confidence in scholastic records is enhanced if the personnel department has required each candidate to request registrars to forward official transcripts directly to the personnel office. They provide information concerning courses taken, dates of attendance, scholastic honors, probation periods if they existed, degrees received, and grades awarded. Placement files may augment data from transcripts by providing information concerning awards, prizes, scholarships, positions held while in school, leadership activities, student offices held, persistent recreational activities. Telephone checking may be indicated with registrars to confirm dates of attendance or with deans, counselors, or professors to secure data concerning a variety of matters: relations with instructors and fellow students; disciplinary action if any was taken; major successes or failures while in school; or an opinion of the position for which the candidate may best be qualified. Further, the state department of education may be asked to confirm the possession of a valid license. All of these data concerning the scholastic record are useful in predicting expected future behavior in academic terms. The validation of work experience needs to be done in terms of actual performance in each prior working situation.

Work Experience

The extent and depth of validation of prior work experience may vary with the category of the position; that is, whether it was a classified, teaching, or administrative position.

Questions common to all three categories may be the following:

Dates of employment.

Position at entry and at the end of the employment period.

Salary at entry and at the end of employment.

Quality of the services rendered.

Regularity of attendance at work.

Relations with fellow employees.

Accidents, if any.

Reason for leaving, if known.

Employers' attitudes toward reemployment.

For teaching positions, additional questions may be:

Kinds of students who fared well under instruction.

Kinds of students who fared worse under instruction.

Relations with parents and the community.

Relations with students.

Relations with nonschool educational agencies.

Relations with other members of the profession.

For administrative positions, additional inquiries may be:

Organizational goal setting behavior.

Experiences in allocating responsibilities to personnel.

Activities in reinforcement and redirection of personnel efforts.

Decision-making habits.

Skills of inquiry concerning organizational problems.

Record-keeping activities.

Potential for coordinating work with nonschool educational agencies.

Communication behaviors.

Personnel skills.

Skills of priority determination and scheduling of activities.

If discrepancies are discovered in the process of validating work experience, they can normally be resolved in the subsequent interview with the candidate. On occasion, however, a discrepancy may surface that requires special inquiry.

Special Validation Inquiries

An unexplained gap in employment, for example, if suggested by other data, may prompt a search in the state criminal records to determine if there has been a period of incarceration. The report of study or work in an uncommon, or defunct, organization may require investigation of its existence or quality. A candidate clearly living beyond his means may prompt the purchase of a credit report. Caution, however, must be used in setting up these special inquiries; they are justified only if routine validation inquiries produce unexplained or contradictory information.

If validation of records produces no surprises, and the records seem to indicate further screening may be profitable, the current skills of the candidate should be confirmed.

Skills Confirmation

Skill confirmation after employment has been, and continues to be, the basis of continuation of employment. But the costs of recruitment, selection, training, and replacement are so onerous that personnel departments have tried to find ways of reducing costs by anticipating the skill potential of candidates. One method tried early (since W.D. Scott developed the first techniques at Northwestern University in 1901)[2] was personnel testing using measuring instruments prepared by industrial psychologists.

Personnel Testing

The use of general tests (that is, intelligence, interests, personality, spatial perception, and information to infer skill potential) was, according to French, brought under fire by personnel directors and others as early as 1955.[3] In 1978, Dyer reported that a U.S. Supreme Court decision (*Griggs* v. *The Duke Power Company*) in 1971 caused many companies to eliminate testing programs altogether. He added that the severity of this ruling had been mitigated somewhat by a section of the Federal Executive Agency's 1976 Guidelines. Indeed, Section 4b did restore permission to use tests to screen out a sizable number of a large group of applicants if "reasonable affirmative action goals are not [thereby] violated."[4] The law defined reasonableness as the employment of four women or minority applicants with each five men or nonminority candidates. Thus, a limited area for testing to enhance recruitment screening does exist.

Testing would seem to be a useful strategy in assessing the knowledge components of skill. This may include, for example, skill options in the resolution of students' learning problems, the choice of tools and materials of instruction, or the definition of parameters of a productive learning environment. It may, further, include an understanding of sequences of skill development, sequences of the use of knowledge in instruction, or coordination of in-school and out-of-school instruction. Items selected for inclusion in such tests should, typically, be directly related to the skills under consideration. Limitations on testing, however, have had the effect of shifting emphasis in skill confirmation to work sampling.

Work Sampling

Work sampling in the selection of nonteaching personnel may be done in the employer's work spaces, using machinery provided by the employer.

Disadvantages related to work sampling may be the inability of the administrator to evaluate reactions such as tension developed because of (1) unfamiliarity with a new tool or procedure, or (2) eagerness to perform well. Yet, a sympathetic discounting of tension may be necessary to evaluate results accurately.

The incorporation of affirmative action procedures into selection has produced a variant of work sampling. The requirements of the Equal Employment Opportunity Commission and the Federal Executive Agency have sometimes led to the employment of individuals with short work histories, minimal skills, or undeveloped potential. Under these circumstances, work sampling may be augmented by instruction, extended over a period of time, and terminated only on evidence of incapacity for developing the desired spectrum of skills. Sometimes probation periods are extended by the length of the threshold training provided. While this procedure is defensible in developing staff diversity, it does not eliminate the possibility of developing tension in the candidates. Under these circumstances, tactful, supporting instruction that provides frequent reinforcement of skill achievement can ameliorate the possible deleterious effects of long trials. Another variation of work sampling and testing incorporated into a fairly cumbersome procedure has been simulation in assessment centers.

Assessment Centers

Sofer reported that assessment center procedures in Britain were modeled after the World War II Officer Selection Boards developed by W.R. Bion and others.[5] Beatty and Schneier described the U.S. evaluative procedures for the selection of employees for the Office of Strategic Services as based on the work of Harvard's Henry A. Murray.[6] Beatty and Schneier reported that "they [assessment centers] can be found in every major industry, in government, and in almost every industrialized nation."[7] Bray and associates suggested that the technique of simulation, augmented by testing and evaluation, was studied most thoroughly by the American Telephone and Telegraph Company.[8] The techniques used at these centers are carefully structured to include psychiatrists, psychologists, and management specialists as evaluators; candidates engage in in-basket exercises, management games, leaderless group discussions, tests of verbal and mathematical reasoning, oral presentations, personality quizzes, interest assessment, reading and comprehension tests, interviews, writing projects, and, perhaps, general knowledge tests. Removed from a normal working situation, the candidate is given simulated work, a simulated social situation, and paper and pencil tests. All strategies are designed to anticipate probable candidates' responses to predetermined work situations, and thereby to secure a host of performance data. It is an expensive method, possibly accessible only to a state department of education, a county schools office, or a very large school district, and its applicability to a skill confirmation process in education is untested. Turning to McMurry once again, a less expensive method of skill confirmation may yield more concrete results.[9] He suggested the development of a performance history.

Performance History

Based on reports of the candidate and data from each prior employer, as well as from former colleagues about the work done and the skills it required, a performance history may be developed. The information from the candidate may be found in the application, its supporting documents, and statements made in a patterned interview. Using the telephone check to verify these data with prior employers and colleagues, attention can be directed to skills that have been demonstrated at work. Upon verification of all data, skills may be classified as "sometimes demonstrated," "repeated frequently," or "seldom practiced." It must be pointed out that there are many weaknesses in this technique: (1) the incompleteness of the telephone check; (2) the reluctance of prior employers to provide data, a natural reticence; (3) the difficulty of securing data from former colleagues; and (4) the variability of interview results. But, in spite of these reservations, the performance history has the unique advantage of directing attention to observed behavior that can, by projection, indicate capabilities in new working situations.

In discussing these alternatives for confirmation of skills, it is not implied that there is a "best" way, or that a completely accurate prediction of skilled performance can be made. In effect, it is suggested that no greater expense than absolutely necessary should be incurred. In selecting persons for a low-skill, high-turnover position, for example, in-house work sampling may be more cost effective than any other procedure.

Even though skills cannot be confirmed readily or completely, their characteristic application in prior working situations presents, in some ways, a simpler problem.

Substantiation of Work Habits

Work habits, unlike skills which may be specific to the tools used, the duties assigned, and the working context, are developed slowly over time and generally persist despite changes in either the working situation or duties assigned. This is true, particulary, of aspirational behavior.

Aspirational Behavior

One indication of aspirational behavior is the amount of physical energy a candidate has been willing to expend at work. It is no secret that some work histories show an ability to carry on quality work for long periods of time without apparent fatigue. Indeed, a person showing this characteristic may be holding successfully two positions in the same or different organizations, carrying on a major occupation while achieving honors in a collegiate career, or performing well in an expanded job normally occupied by two persons. High-energy employees are more apt to recognize problems ignored by others, persist in their solution, and challenge others to assist them. Concomitantly, such individuals may be at odds with those who run on a different schedule; that is, low-aspirational employees who, among other things, may use some of the energy they do expend in strenuous efforts to reject problems.

Schutz and associates identified techniques directed at problem rejection as (1) reluctance to admit the presence of a problem, (2) admiring it as a problem without becoming involved in its solution, (3) identifying it as someone else's problem, (4) excusing noninvolvement on the grounds of inexperience, (5) accepting full responsibility without action, and (6) rationalization of the problem into one that NO ONE can resolve.[10] Other characteristics of problem rejectors include frequent changes of employment, of occupations, of places to live, and of spouses. Interestingly enough, some of these characteristics make the problem rejectors appear to be individuals who prize independence.

Truly independent men and women, however, have work histories that include finding their own positions, achieving youthful fiscal independence, seeking decision-making opportunities, expressing opinions contrary to the majority, and preferring one-person assignments. To use Carlson's terms, genuine independents are more likely to be "career bound" than "place bound."[11] Place boundness is suggested by a history that includes acceptance of leadership of student affairs, voluntary associations, social groups, professional organizations, and working units. It may be described as a process of "setting down roots" to facilitate advancement in a chosen social and organizational setting.

As for female employees, it may well be that social custom has long cast women into restrictive roles in teaching, retail selling, and clerical work. Lately, affirmative action has partially opened the door to a much larger spectrum of employment. Whether that larger spectrum of work will be filled by female employees may well depend on the extent to which they can overcome a self-restraining tendency, described by social scientists as reluctance to move from the classic occupations because of a fear of nonacceptance of successful performance in other fields. It may be that, today, women employees' desire to achieve may offset their fear of inadequate reinforcement. In line with this thinking, special attention should be paid in the preparation of work histories for women to their (1) persistence at work, (2) levels of accomplishment, and (3) success achieved under differing conditions.

But the determination of aspirational behavior is only one aspect of work habits that deserve attention in fine screening. Most work is done in groups; habits of group participation are significant. McMurry has termed these "products of motivations."

Motivations

Eight different types of group behavior have been described by McMurry as products of motivation:

The need for income;

The need for security;

Desire for status;

The need for power;

Satisfaction of curiosity;

Competitiveness;

Perfectionism; and

A desire to serve.[12]

Although a great deal of speculation, inference, and anecdotal data may be required to substantiate any or all of these patterns of behavior, they are fairly clear and recognizable indicators of the motivations that generated them. The need for income is sometimes the easiest to substantiate.

Need for Income

The most evident manifestation of the need for income is the lifestyle of the applicant (that is, comforts required, clothing worn, cars driven, luxuries valued, houses possessed, recreations sought, schools and colleges attended by the applicant and his offspring, and avocational interests). Often the financial burdens accepted (for example, support of other members of an extended family) may indicate needs for income. Another visible indication may be a willingness to engage in a high-risk position that pays high wages. Sometimes a willingness to engage in multiple occupations at the same time may be significant. The willingness to engage in high-risk occupations may differentiate the income-needy applicant from the one who seeks security.

Need for Security

Applicants who place high value on security characteristically select low-risk occupations definable as having fairly obscure standards of employee performance, perfunctory personnel evaluations, and tenure after a relatively undisturbed probation period. Their work histories are replete with instances of compliant behavior in interacting with individuals perceived to be threats to security (for example, students, parents, community leaders, administrators, or colleagues). It is not unusual for the work history to reveal aggressive, self-protective episodes when a perceived threat places too much stress on the candidate. The behavior displayed by the security seekers contrasts sharply with that of those who value high status or approval.

Desire for Status

Status-seeking behavior may be exhibited by any category of educational personnel. Status-seeking by teachers in the classroom may take the form of constant references to schools attended, honors and degrees received, and publications. In self-reports of intellectual contests with colleagues, the teacher is usually depicted as the hero. The extent of status-seeking in the classroom may range from sacrificing the rigor of intellectual inquiry to entertaining the students to gain approval.

Educational personnel seeking status in the community choose another path. It often leads to the acceptance of multiple, demanding, but prestigious voluntary positions in the many organizations with which the candidate has been affiliated.

Status-seeking in the profession can usually be noted by a constant, visible battle to achieve advanced degrees or elective positions. Administrators have been known to become walking data banks producing detailed data concerning school operations to demonstrate command of the organizational problems. Other manifestations are development of public speaking skills (often used to deliver many humorous addresses to service clubs). Further manifestations include book publication, as long as those published are popular. It can be said that those who seek approval are hoping for reassurance. It follows, then, that those who need power have assurance in abundance.

The Need for Power

Power oriented candidates, for most educational posts, reveal a fairly consistent pattern of behavior. If they are classroom teachers, they are apt to have been authoritative in classroom management. They are likely to have been grudging in accepting student suggestions for modifications of goals or instructional procedures, defensive in responding to student challenges, and quick to discipline students reluctant to accept the tasks assigned.

If they are administrators, they will have been rigorous in establishing organizational structure, firm in requiring loyalty of subordinates, and quick to evaluate and discipline nonconformists. In community and professional affairs, power-oriented candidates are less likely to have sought elected positions than surreptitious insertion of themselves into the committees and informal structures that determine those who are to be nominated and elected. Many such candidates display a strong personal commitment to the manipulation of others by acceptance of propaganda procedures in securing public action, operant conditioning in classroom instruction, or stern discipline in all organizational operations. The self-assurance of the power oriented is in sharp contrast to those who value the satisfaction of curiosity.

Satisfaction of Curiosity

Curiosity may be said to be a significant characteristic of a candidate when there is evidence of the suspension of judgment until facts are available, a commitment to inquiry including experimentation, and persistence in resolving ambiguity in organizational operations by recourse to theory and evidence. A candidate will have displayed curiosity when there are episodes showing attempts to disseminate results of his investigations to colleagues and the public, instances of his having challenged, by evidence or reason, the uncritical acceptance of goals and procedures, or efforts directed at resolving professional problems encountered by his colleagues. Whether any of these efforts proved successful is not the issue here; however, the effectiveness of the candidate evidencing curiosity is enhanced if he has demonstrated a high degree of competitiveness as well.

Competitiveness

Competitive behavior is characterized by the willingness of the candidate to sacrifice his time, effort, and even his dignity to win a contest. For example, he may persist in practice of difficult skills until he masters them more completely than others. To practice, he may add consultation with experts to secure evaluations for the improvement of fine skills to improve performance. He may persist in inquiry to discover the most appropriate procedures for problem resolution, develop creative or unique ways for solving stubborn organizational problems, or insist on post mortems to analyze the causes of failure. Competitive behavior may include "team loyalty," that is, a willingness to sacrifice personal recognition in the interest of organizational success. Competitiveness carried to its extreme may lead to perfectionism.

Perfectionism

In work histories, perfectionism will show up as an unswerving attention to detail. Episodes will show negative reactions to failures of colleagues to follow standard procedures. They will show among teachers of composition, for example, an emphasis on spelling and punctuation that may cause a neglect of the ideas being communicated. Among administrators, they may display a preoccupation with records and reports to the exclusion of considerations of purpose and function. They may show, as well, a necessary attention to detail to assure the completion of a complicated task. But perfectionism may have been developed in order to satisfy a desire for service.

Desire to Serve

The desire to serve appears in work histories as selflessness. Among teachers, there may have been episodes in which, from limited funds, they have provided books, clothing, or food to students in need. They may have been willing to spend many extra hours in counseling students with difficulties or parents with problem children. They may have been willing personally to finance periods of intensive study in order to serve students more adequately. But selflessness may have taken the form of attachment to great causes also (for example, a personal commitment to union leadership, strong participation in a feminist movement, an undying commitment to democracy or some other political philosophy, or a religious fervor for the redemption of mankind). And selflessness may have taken the form of lifetime care of an aged parent, the sole support of a large family, or the care of an incompetent child.

These motivational behaviors, combined with evidence of aspirational behavior, provide data to determine persistent work habits of candidates. If a perception of work habits is added to data concerning skills and information from records, the only information lacking to complete a work history and permit fine screening is the candidates' reactions to prior working assignments. These can be secured efficiently by use of a patterned interview.

Candidate Reactions to Prior Assignments: The Patterned Interview

A patterned interview can serve as a culmination of the preparation of the work history by (1) resolving ambiguities created by other evidence, (2) examining the candidate's persistent responses to successive working situations, (3) reviewing the candidate's reactions to former colleagues, and (4) determining the candidate's satisfactions with each working assignment. Because it is a culminative activity, the interviewer should have reviewed all data in the work history prior to the interview. And he should enter the interview with a set of printed questions (cues) included in a form that provides space to record a summary of the candidate's responses.

The Patterned Interview

The interview should be conducted with some cautions in mind. Since it may require an hour or more, privacy and comfort are essential. Responses should not be shortened by time restraints, unusual reactions by the interviewer, or sales pitches for the employer. All questions and cues should be presented in a conversational tone. Responses should not be interrupted save for prompting to secure additional necessary detail. The list of cues should be presented to the candidate for each work experience. Military experience is properly treated as a work assignment. Requests for explanation of discrepancies in records or responses should be made with the assumption that a rational reason exists. The interview should not be terminated because the interviewer, or the candidate, has decided that the application for the candidacy is futile. It should not be terminated until both feel that the candidate has had full opportunity to give his reactions. if these precautions are taken, the success of the interview may depend upon the quality of the cues used by the interviewer.

An example of a set of cues that may be used in interviewing candidates for educational positions follows. They were adapted from cues recommended by McMurry for use in patterned interviews of candidates for executive positions in industry. They are:

Why did you choose the position?

What promotions did you receive while you worked there?

What did you do in each position?

What kind of supervisor(s) did you have?

What kind of people worked with you?

What did you especially like in your assignment(s)?

What did you dislike the most?

To what extent did you control your assignment?

To what extent did you participate in policymaking?

To what extent were you able to exercise initiative and judgment?

What did your family think of your assignment(s)?

Why did you leave (or stay)?

Would you be willing to work there again (or stay to retirement)?[13]

There is, of course, no magic to this particular set of cues; others may serve as well, depending upon the organization and its need for information about the candidate. Regardless of specific cues chosen, the purpose of the interview will be lost if the interviewer has failed to anticipate the possible meanings of the responses given. One important set of responses relates to persistence with the same employer.

Persistence with the Same Employer

There are a number of reasons to be kept in mind why people remain with one employer or organization. Chief among these are: (1) they were satisfied with the assignment or really enjoyed the associations with their colleagues, (2) they were place bound and determined to get ahead within the organization, (3) they were unable to find another position with the same or equivalent compensation, or (4) there was security in the yearly repetition of familiar routines. Yet other employees changed employers for just as many—or more—good reasons. Among these are: (1) they were following a planned career development; (2) they found new challenges stimulating; (3) their spouses had changed employers; (4) there were economic pressures which forced them to find more adequate salaries; (5) their incompetence produced frequent job changes; (6) collegial, community, or administrative criticism made the position unbearable; or (7) they failed to receive satisfying reinforcement for their work. Another reason may have been the assessment of the job as "requiring too much work." Employees' self-evaluation concerning their own industry is worthy of exploration.

Industry

A candidate's report of spending excessive hours in a prior assignment—a not uncommon response from candidates for educational positions—may be attributed to (1) inequitable assignments, (2) assignment of tasks for which the candidate was ill prepared, or (3) voluntary acceptance of ancillary duties not included in the work required. Yet, reports of procrastination in completing, or neglect of, assigned tasks may be rooted in such familiar personnel problems as (1) imperfect role designations, (2) poor supervision, or (3) lack of student or collegial cooperation. Self-evaluated diligence may also be attributed to other reasons, such as (1) fear of discipline, (2) emotional attachment to personally valued goals, (3) concern for career advancement, or (4) fear of collegial criticism. As discussed in a preceding section, voluntarism in seeking and accepting ancillary duties may have been prompted by needs for income, security, approval, power, curiosity, perfectionism, competitiveness, or service. But reported lack of attention to assigned tasks may have been caused by (1) poor health, (2) boredom, (3) confusion about assignments, (4) lack of confidence in colleagues or the organization, or (5) despair about student behavior. Industry, however, may be related closely to satisfaction with the assignment.

Satisfaction with the Assignment

Herzberg's thesis about the motivations to work, which preceded McMurry's definition of motivations by almost a decade, suggested that reports of satisfaction with assignments may be attributed to opportunities to achieve, recognition by others, the fascination with the work itself, responsibility assigned and accepted, and the opportunity for advancement. Herzberg and associates, however, pointed out that the absence of these characteristics in the assignment did not necessarily lead to dissatisfaction. Dissatisfaction stemmed from (1) salaries received; (2) the absence of the possibility for growth; (3) interpersonal relations with subordinates, superiors, or peers; (4) status contrary to expectations; (5) inadequate supervision; (6) disagreements with organizational policies; (7) uncomfortable or dangerous working conditions; (8) personal life difficulties; and (9) job insecurity.[14]

In view of the multitude of possible interpretations, prudence suggests an exploration of these dimensions of satisfaction in each previous assignment both with the candidate in the patterned interview and with supervisors and colleagues following it. In the exploration of satisfaction with colleagues, some data may be gathered concerning the habits of interaction with them.

Interactions with Colleagues

Candidate reports of interactions with colleagues may need to be interpreted by examining the clarity of role definitions in the work unit (that is, unit definition of tasks, their assignment to individuals in terms of levels of responsibility, prior definition of individuals to be consulted or informed, and the utility of means provided for resolution of collegial conflicts). If the unit work plan provides no explanations of reported collegial interaction, attention may need to be directed to the motivational behavior of the candidate or his colleagues that fosters or impedes interactions. If these explanations are inadequate, attention may be directed to the organizational policies that affect the possibility of interaction (that is, fragmentation of work units, geographic isolation of units, administrative styles, emphasis on entrepreneuring, or power distributions among colleagues).

Keeping all data from the work history in mind, listening intently to the responses of the candidate, and remembering the working context into which the new employee is to be placed, the interviewer should attempt to identify persistent work behavior by using what may be termed the "rolling hypothesis" technique. In doing this, he hypothesizes the reasons for prior behavior, amending the hypothesis as new responses are given, discarding it when it becomes unsupportable, and developing another more compatible with the data given. If the hypothesis proves tenable, he documents it further by new responses. If substantial support for hypotheses formed during the interview is lacking at its end, further evidence may be sought from sources already established. But the final result of the fine screening process should be a report to the unit administrator that predicts, within the limits of available evidence, the probable behavior of each candidate in the work unit.

Fine Screening Reports

A fine screening report that performs this service should, therefore, address the following appointment consequences:

Challenges to the unit staff's educational values consensus that may result.

Skills and knowledge to be added to staff resources by the appointment.

Responsibilities for the candidate's skill development that may need to be assumed by the staff.

Modifications in staff collegial interactions that may result.

Predicted persistence in the assignment, if appointed.

Summary

The fine screening of selection is a process of developing a validated work history for each candidate chosen in recruiting. This is done to permit the personnel department to predict, within the limits of evidence available, the probable behavior of each in the work unit. The accuracy of the prediction depends upon the completeness of the evidence available concerning the following:

Skills demonstrated in prior assignments.

Knowledge utilized.

Aspirational behavior displayed.

Motivational behavior.

Persistent work habits.

Characteristic reactions to colleagues and assignments.

These data are secured from applications, transcripts, patterned interviews, telephone checks with preparing institutions and former employers, and testing as appropriate. They are used to prepare predictions that estimate unit gains to be achieved by the appointment of each, identify unit problems likely to be created, and display anticipated reactions of each candidate to colleagues and the assignment. Using these predictions, the unit administrator is expected to select the candidate who could staff a preferred unit work plan.

Notes

1. Robert N. McMurry, *Tested Techniques of Personnel Selection* (Chicago: The Dartnell Corporation, 1966), section 4, pp. 7-12.

2. Cyril Sofer, *Organizations in Theory and Practice* (New York: Basic Books, 1972), pp. 51-52.

3. Wendell French, *The Personnel Management Process* (Boston: Houghton Mifflin, 1964), pp. 140-148.

4. Frank J. Dyer, "An Alternative to Validating Selection Tests," *Personnel Journal* 57 (1978):200-203.

5. Sofer, *Organizations*, pp. 194-215.

6. Richard W. Beatty and Craig E. Schneier, *Personnel Administration* (Menlo Park, Calif.: Addison-Wesley, 1977), p. 222.

7. Ibid., pp. 222-227.

8. D.W. Bray et al. *Formative Years in Business: A Long Term Study of Managerial Lives* (New York: John Wiley, 1974).

9. McMurry, *Personnel Selection*, section 5, pp. 1-4.

10. William C. Schutz et al., *Procedures for Identifying Persons with Potential for Public School Administrative Positions* (Berkeley: University of California Graduate School of Education, 1961), U.S. Office of Education Cooperative Research Project No. 677, p. 178.

11. Richard O. Carlson, *Executive Succession and Organizational Change* (Chicago: Midwest Administration Center, University of Chicago, 1962).

12. McMurry, *Personnel Selection*, section 7, pp. 1-10.

13. Ibid., section 5, exhibit 4.

14. Frederick Herzberg, Bernard Mausner, and Barbara Snyderman, *The Motivation to Work* (New York: John Wiley, 1959).

5 Assignment and Transfer

It is obviously beyond the bounds of reason—and it is self-defeating—to employ an individual for, or transfer him to, an assignment without taking every possible organizational act aimed at giving him a chance to succeed. Whatever the existing differences between systems of management thought, their advocates have all developed recommendations concerning (1) employee motivation, (2) role definition, (3) collegial interaction, and (4) conflict resolution. But because the differences between the systems lie in the perspective from which each views the employee and his relations to the organization, procedures adopted have varied according to the perspective.

Scientific Administration Assignment Policies and Procedures

The scientific administration concept of management viewed the employee as an entrepreneur; thus, in the scientific administrators' development of assignment policies, they emphasized the employee's competitiveness in reaching for economic rewards.

Motivation

Endorsing economic motivation, the scientific administrators adopted Taylor's (1911) plan for piece-rate pay. Taylor suggested that employees could become "high pay" employees by producing more units than the standard set for an average day's work. In other words, Taylor advocated outperforming fellow workers in the pursuit of enlightened self-interest. To assist each worker in the development of this kind of performance, many steps were taken by the organization. In line with this thinking, early personnel activities aimed at this result were developed. Employees had to be selected with care to assure they had the skill potential to do the work. Once hired, the employees had to be taught the "best way" to get the work done. Tools had to be designed to fit the unique talents of the employee. Administrators had to revise work standards periodically in order to keep abreast of current definitions of a reasonable day's work. The school administrators who subscribed to the scientific administration system adapted these economic motivation concepts by instituting the idea of "merit pay."

But school administrators could not adopt fully the economic motivation concept. In 1923, almost a decade after Taylor's theories received great public support, the National Education Association endorsed the single salary schedule. As a consequence, merit pay practices declined both in favor and number within public school systems, thus making it impossible to outperform anyone for reasons of economic gain. The standards concept, however, was not entirely abandoned. In fact, administrators developed and used annual tests to determine productivity and efficiency of teachers. Nor did educational administrators abandon the scientific administration view of employee role definition.

Role Definition

School system roles were defined by bureaucratic titles. As every educational placement officer can testify, requests for personnel still come in for a "primary teacher," an "intermediate grades teacher," a "tenth grade English teacher," a "social studies teacher," or, perhaps, a "wood shop teacher." More simplistic still, in many instances, no supplementary data were provided, on the evident assumption that none was needed. Definition of roles by title has been reinforced by state licensing systems that classify certificates by these labels. Clearly, with the exception of some minor adaptations, such practices of school administrators and licensing authorities mirror the procedures developed by scientific administrators working in business and industry.

But school administrators subscribing to the tenets of scientific administration adopted more than merely standards and bureaucratic titles; they quickly agreed that planning (policy) should be separated from action (administration). Specialization and division of labor concepts were used not only to separate secondary instruction into "disciplines," but to define elementary grades by the ages of students. Productivity was defined in terms of student gains on standarized tests. And the concept of treating employees impersonally was not unpopular among school administrators. In this type of organizational climate, it was no wonder that the scientific administration concept of collegiality was negative—and unrelated.

Collegial Interaction

Collegiality was perhaps most succinctly defined for the system by Taylor himself:

> When workmen are herded together in gangs, each man in the gang becomes far less efficient than when his personal ambition is stimulated . . . when men work in gangs, their individual ambition falls almost invariably down to or below the level of the worst man in the gang . . . they are all pulled down instead of being elevated by being herded together.[1]

He continued:

> the few misplaced drones, who do the loafing and [under group incentive schemes] share equally in the profits with the rest, under cooperation are sure to drag the better men down toward their level.[2]

In one experimental assignment scheme conducted by Taylor, he separated women workers by seating them so far apart that they could not talk to each other. This emphasis on individual enterprise led to a "disciplinary" concept of conflict resolution.

Conflict Resolution

The disciplinary system of the scientific administrators was anchored in the duty of management to maintain the integrity of the work plan. Again, it was Taylor who defined it most clearly: "It is only through enforced standardization of methods, enforced adoption of the best implements and working conditions, and enforced cooperation that this faster work can be assured."[3]

This authoritarian concept of discipline caused employees to be dismissed if they could not negotiate with management disagreements over assignments, methods of work, disputes with fellow workmen, standards of production, tools of production, rates of pay, or working conditions. And it was this disciplinary concept of conflict resolution that contributed more than any other practice to the development of human relations concepts in the 1930s.

Human Relations Administration Assignment Policies and Procedures

The human relations concept of management viewed the employee as a member of a group, something akin to a fraternal order. Emphasizing democracy in organizational leadership, its main exponent was Kurt Lewin, a German gestalt psychologist, who emigrated to the United States in 1933 and worked in this country until his death fifteen years later. At that time, Lewin was the director of the Research Center for Group Dynamics,

Massachusetts Institute of Technology. Gordon Allport, in his foreword to a collection of the psychologist's essays edited by his wife after his death, evaluated Lewin's contribution to human relations concepts as follows:

> Lewin has been called the "outstanding psychological exponent" of democracy. More clearly than anyone else has he shown us in concrete terms what it means to be a democratic leader and to create a democratic group structure.[4]

Following Lewin's lead, human relations policies and procedures emphasized group controls and participation in motivating employees.

Motivation

The most powerful motivating force, according to the human relation theorists, was the desire to maintain group identity. Lewin stated this premise as follows:

> [An employee must anchor his] conduct in something as large, substantial, and super-invididual as the culture of a group . . . to stabilize his new beliefs sufficiently to keep them immune from day to day fluctuations of moods and influences, to which he, as an individual, is subject.[5]

Or, as he also said:

> The experiments on success and failure, level of aspiration, intelligence, frustration, and all the others have shown more and more convincingly that a goal a person sets for himself is deeply influenced by the social standards of the group to which he belongs or wishes to belong.[6]

Teachers throughout the United States were quick to accept this group definition of motivation, perhaps because of the almost unanimous acceptance of scientific administration tenets by administrators.

The National Education Association cooperated fully with the Research Center for Group Dynamics at the Massachusetts Institute of Technology to create and supply Participants for the National Training Laboratory at Bethel, Maine. In 1950, Gunderson described the three-week session at Bethel as follows:

> The National Training Laboratory on Group Development . . . has met for the past three summers in Bethel, Maine. For three weeks each summer 150 persons described as "key education and action leaders" have met for a "workshop" in group dynamics.[7]

The NEA participation in the National Training Laboratory was, perhaps, a culmination of teachers' preoccupation with democracy in schools, which began with John Dewey of Teachers College, Columbia University, in 1916. This perspective of education reached its peak in the early 1930s as Dewey's ideas were publicized in the writings of Boyd Bode of Ohio State University and William Heard Kilpatrick of Teachers College, Columbia University.

The broad interest in democracy and democratic group participation sounded the death knell of the rather simplistic scientific administration reliance on economic motivation as the prime mover of employees. But in placing emphasis on group participation, the human relations advocates encountered difficulty in assisting individuals to find their places in groups.

Role Definition

The search for role definition within a democratic group generated a new field of inquiry. "Group dynamics" asked how an individual participated democratically in a group;" it searched for and found collective and individual roles defined in the new field of social psychology, which, understandably, had developed at the same time. Four role classifications were borrowed and redefined by Gibbs and Gibbs. As reported by Bennis and Shepard as the most comprehensive, these roles were defined as follows:

> Task Roles: Initiating activity; seeking information; seeking opinion; giving information; giving opinion; elaborating; coordinating; summarizing; testing feasibility.
>
> Group Maintenance Roles: Encouraging; gate keeping; standard setting; following; expressing group feelings.
>
> Task and Group Roles: Evaluating; diagnosing; testing for consensus; mediating; relieving tension.
>
> Individual Roles: Being aggressive; blocking; self-confessing; commenting; seeking sympathy; special pleading; horsing around; seeking recognition; withdrawing.[8]

Please note that all descriptors of these role definitions are used in the progressive tense, as befits the "action" implied in the term "dynamic."

As can be seen from the category headings, finding a definition of role for the individual within the group was not enough; there was also concern for the maintenance of the group itself. In this inquiry, it was established that a group was often composed of many informal parts, called primary units, and that membership in these face-to-face groups could be beneficial, as well as detrimental, to group maintenance. Thus role definition in the human relations system of mangement went beyond task definition to account for problems of collegiality and cooperation.

Even though teachers were interested in, and supportive of, the human relations system of administration, school administrators were forced by circumstances to give it little more than lip service. This was caused by the peaking of interest in the system of administrative thought in the 1930s and 1940s, a time etched in American minds as that related to the Great Depression, a period in which schools were so poorly supported that the earlier virtues of productivity and efficiency seemed more suitable. It was also the period before and during World War II, in which many of the more traditional values of academic training had to make way for a responsive and responsible method to deal with the problems of total war. Primary among these problems were (1) shortages of teaching personnel, (2) the necessity to create new schools in war production areas, and (3) vocational preparation of an expanded workforce. The scientific administration virtues of productivity and efficiency were valued more highly than democracy in group participation.

But even if political, social, and economic conditions had been more favorable to the human relations system of management, it is doubtful that school administrators would have been eager to adopt it. They were, for the most part, graduates of schools of education that were just organizing, or had just organized, administrative studies curricula modeled after the programs at Teachers College, Columbia University; Stanford; University of Chicago; and Yale. And these programs for the preparation of administrators had been founded by professors committed to scientific administration. They were Ellwood Cubberley at Stanford, George Strayer at Columbia, Francis Spaulding at Yale, and Franklin Bobbitt at Chicago. Having been taught administration in terms of scientific procedures, administrators in the 1930s and 1940s made concessions to the current teachers' enthusiasms for human relations by adopting largely cosmetic concessions to the idea (that is, horizontal, vertical, and administrative committees; frequent faculty meetings; and consultative management which seemed always to translate out to mean that committee decisions could always be overturned by administrative fiat). These concessions enabled administrators to maintain bureaucratic role definitions, but never produced the collegiality and democratic group participation contemplated by Lewin and Dewey.

Collegial Interaction

For clearly it was collegiality, defined as democratic group participation, which constituted the core of the human relations system of management thought. Because it viewed motivation as a process of group conformity, it contemplated role definition as a fluid process of contributing whatever an individual could to the group-determined work activities. In this concept, conflict resolution was viewed as a necessary adjunct of group participation.

Conflict Resolution

Conflict was viewed as constructive, and inevitable, a profitable product of collegial interaction. Perhaps Mary Parker Follett's views on conflict resolution had the most impact on management theorists. In a paper published in 1926 she disposed of dominance and compromise as ineffective ways of resolving conflict. Dominance by administrators or others resolved the problem quickly, in her opinion, but created problems later. In using compromise, both parties, she said, had to give up something; they always tended to ask too much because they knew this. She endorsed "integration," a method of resolving conflict that called for both sides to find a place for their desires, without a sacrifice by either.[9] It required conflict to be openly exposed to examine the motives and desires of the contestants. The consequent open discussion was expected to cause contestants to modify values, thereby causing realignments of groups and changing the nature of the conflict. In Follett's opinion, this would strengthen group action by providing more tenable alternatives for decision choices. It would serve also to broaden the group value consensus.

Ironically, it was precisely the human relations system's focus on the group which led to its downfall as a popular theory of management. It is possible to speculate, from today's vantage point, that an attachment to a single group represents an anomaly in an ever-expanding, complex, metropolitan, industrial society. Employees in a work unit, surely, belong to many groups. The organization itself is but a subsystem of a much larger social system. Indeed, single-minded, defensive attachment to one work group within a large organization may produce organizational chaos. It may be said without fear of exaggeration that organizational chauvinism is a recipe for social anarchy.

Thus, gradually, the growing realization of the impossibility of establishing any legal, organizational, or societal mechanism for resolving the endless and inevitable conflicts among groups led to the development of the social systems management theory.

Social System Administration Assignment Policies and Procedures

In social systems management, the employee is viewed as a goal seeker. It is said that he "believes" that certain ends (goals) should be reached. It is an administrative approach that believes the employee recognizes there are organizational, professional, and societal limitations to the accomplishment of all ends that he believes are essential, but that he is willing to persist as long as there is promise of eventual fulfillment. A markedly different view of the employee from either the scientific (economic) or the human relations (group participation) concept, it involves a concept of motivation as self-fulfillment.

Motivation

Both Maslow, in discussing the hierarchy of human motives,[10] and Herzberg, in elaborating "satisfiers,"[11] emphasized self-fulfillment as the most powerful motive, although neither was concerned about the management procedures that might be used to assure it. And the social psychologists who provided much of the terminology about beliefs, goals, and values used by social systems theorists (Rokeach, Allport, Festinger, many others) were not interested in management procedures. But the last named, being interested in group processes, did provide clues that can be used to develop management procedures.

Following Rokeach's definition of beliefs, explained in chapter 2, an employee entering a work group for the first time came with attitudes (a disposition to take certain actions) justified in terms of hierarchies of terminal and instrumental values (a view of the desirable end state he valued). These beliefs were uniquely his because they had been developed by experience in different groups and work situations. Since they were unique, the entry of the new work group member provided continuing members an opportunity to reexamine their beliefs by comparing them to those of the newcomer. The employee should, therefore, have an opportunity to challenge the beliefs of the members of the work group he was joining. If Rokeach and McLellan were correct in their conclusions (also described in chapter 2), this challenge-response dialogue would produce two desirable results: (1) the newcomer could reconstruct his belief system to the extent that he could work cooperatively with the members of the group, and (2) the group could modify its belief system to more nearly accommodate the motivated effort of the newcomer.

But educational beliefs are not often congruent with the goals of the work unit. Goals are usually that portion of what ought to be done that can be accomplished within the constraints placed upon the work unit. These constraints are societal, organizational, and professional. No work group can for long persist in instruction that the supporting community believes should not be done. If the members of the work group persist, the community will deny it financial support, insist on personnel changes, or withdraw students from the school. No work group can continue instructional activities that are alien to its role assignment in the school system. The penalties for aberrant behavior include loss of personnel, space, and financial support. But, most of all, the work unit cannot perform educational services for which professional skills are in short supply. Sometimes the optimism of strong belief persuades the members of a work group that they can learn by doing. Too often this optimism turns to bitterness in the ashes of failure, a result that might have been anticipated if there had been a serious review of the state of the art. Thus the selection of goals from among those that might assure full realization of educational beliefs requires intent examination of evidence concerning professional, organizational, and community restraints.

These limitations on the choice of goals may provoke different responses from different kinds of newcomers to the work unit. The most extreme is rejection of the assignment and an early request for transfer. The most common is grousing about limited goals. Often this takes the form of grumbling and dissatisfaction classified by Herzberg as objections to superiors, peers, technical supervision, school policies, and working conditions. Sometimes organizational dissatisfaction is projected and becomes the cause of personal problems of health, marriage, or relations with friends.[12] The most desired reaction is acceptance of limitations with hope. Selznick describes the beneficial effects of acceptance as follows: "The in-building of purposes is a challenge to creativity because it involves transforming men and groups from neutral, technical units into participants who have a peculiar stamp, sensitivity, and commitment."[13]

The adoption of these motivational procedures requires the assignment of tasks compatible with the motives of the employee. Role definition, therefore, is less fluid than in human relations system of management thought, but more group-oriented than in scientific administration.

Role Definition

Since goal seeking is the rationale, role definition directs prime attention to task assignment; the tasks assigned are subgoals. This development of role definition creates problems that often confound the cooperative effort of the personnel department and the unit administrator. The state of the art, at times, is too underdeveloped to identify usable subgoals. The personnel available may not be motivated to accept and complete essential tasks. Members of the staff may be motivated to complete the same tasks, and the ones they prefer may occupy only a narrow spectrum of all the work that should be done. Motivated staff members may possess too few essential skills. The tasks that should be completed are, at times, too many for the staff that are available. The resolution of these problems requires the personnel department and the unit administrator to cope with the following problems: (1) the definition of a reasonable day or week's work, (2) differentiation of assignments for individuals with varying levels of skill, (3) the motivation of the unmotivated, and (4) task reconstruction as the state of the art grows.

The definition of a reasonable work assignment requires information concerning the normal time required to complete each assigned task. If, for example, an English teacher is assigned the task of reading, correcting, and criticizing 150 short student papers per week, role definition should take into account the usual ten minutes used on each that adds up to 1,500 minutes—twenty-five hours—per week. It should be noted that this kind of work is more easily completed outside the classroom. And the time required for completing this task may vary in different kinds of classes. Papers from a multilingual group of students may require more time than the average. Failure to take task completion times into account may risk task rejection.

An assigned role that requires its occupant to work more than his colleagues, or longer than the accustomed work week in the community, may be modified by neglect. Collegial or family pressures may cause the employee to decide consciously or unconsciously—and perhaps even with a feeling of guilt—which portion of his weekly assignment can be postponed, abandoned, or completed with minimum effort. An earnest, conscientious attempt to complete assigned tasks regardless of the time involved may cause neglect of collegial activity, family, participation in other groups, and work quality to the point of revulsion. All these reactions are destructive of goal accomplishment, and consequently destructive of an opportunity to achieve self-fulfillment.

But self-fulfillment is also frustrated by the assignment of tasks that are too difficult. The experimentation required to develop a new and different skill is time-consuming. Many experiments end in only partial success, which may be interpreted as failure. And the sense of failure is often reinforced by fatigue developed in conceiving, conducting, and evaluating the experiment. The avoidance of these possible results requires tasks to be within the skill range of the employee. But even care in assigning appropriate tasks may not assure self-fulfillment, particularly if they are required of an unmotivated employee.

And it is common to assign tasks to skilled, but unmotivated, personnel when the work must be completed by the staff available. When this is necessary, two alternatives are open to the unit administrator. He can appeal to group loyalty—a powerful motivation in its own right—or he can appeal to professional pride. The use of either may be recognized by both the unit administrator and the employee as a substitution for intrinsic motivation. But this conscious action is an expedient recognized by both as necessary to secure persistence in task completion. If the challenge-response dialogue about educational values does not soon achieve a modification of the employee's beliefs about the tasks to be completed, it would seem that the task assignments should be amended soon to include more that are valued. This is feasible because changes in task assignments are frequent in a dynamic, goal-oriented work unit.

Task assignments require reexamination when (1) a new member joins the work unit; (2) a continuing member develops new capabilities; (3) age, illness, or accident modifies the capabilities of one or more members of the staff; (4) new goals are adopted by the unit; or (5) a member resigns. These reviews of task assignments not only provide opportunities to assign tasks according to motivations, but permit redistributions of work loads, revision of patterns of staff interaction, and modification of levels of responsibility. These actions are essential to the maintenance of collegial interaction.

Collegial Interaction

Collegial interaction is necessary as unit goals and subgoals are clarified and task assignments reveal the coordination required for goal accomplishment. This dynamic process quickly demonstrates that a subgoal is often assigned to more than one person in the work unit. Some one person may be asked to accept and complete the task; another may be asked to see that it is done; and still another may be given oversight over a group of tasks that includes the subgoal. Three or more people may be involved; a failure of one to understand his role may create conflict that endangers task completion. If "everyone's business" is not to become "no one's business," collegial interaction must resolve the conflict. But it should do more than reduce role conflict; it may be the prime source for skill development.

The most common informal practice in skill development is to ask a colleague how to complete an unfamiliar task. The most common response is to give an answer, even if uninformed. It would seem, therefore, that colleagues be identified who are willing, and can, provide assistance in skill development. This group practice would appear to serve three organizational purposes:

Secure broader agreement on tested procedures.

Provide supervisory service at the time of need.

Maintain the cohesion of the work group as a goal seeking unit.

One of the strengths of the voluntary call for collegial assistance is the credibility of a colleague known to have been successful at completing the task. A credible colleague may induce changes in skilled behavior that would not occur if suggested, or even demanded, by someone else in the organization. And the mutual respect fostered by common action for the development of skills reinforces the common search for appropriate goals.

Indeed, common group goals are the product of collegial interaction. Isolated in classrooms, and seldom inspected either by a supervisor or administrator, a teacher often teaches what he thinks is needed by the students. The statement, "You can hire a teacher to teach what you please, but he will have to teach what he knows," may be a truism, but it is accurate. Common group goals are, therefore, more likely to be produced by a collegial challenge-response diaglogue concerning what ought to be done. The criteria for choosing what ought to be done are drawn from the value systems of the participants. When a unit member cannot justify the worth of what he is doing, he will modify either what he is doing or his justification for it. Educational beliefs thus produced are seldom held by the entire membership of the work unit. The more likely distribution is 30 percent agreement, 40 percent disagreement, and 30 percent compliant but neutral. This makes any belief system dynamic, and goals transitory. Under these conditions, collegial challenge-response becomes essential. But it can be impaired by formal or informal status allocations within the work group.

The most formal status designations in working groups are administrative. When principals, counselors, department heads, or other group leaders are given veto powers that can only be described as omnipotent, collegial interaction is diminished to the extent that vetos are arbitrary, impulsive, or self-serving. This does not rule out the need for administrators who occupy the indispensable role of coordinator of many, often conflicting, energetic, productive members of the unit. It does rule out the imperial, all-knowing administrator. But informal status allocations are equally destructive of collegial interaction.

In colleges and universities, for example, restriction of promotion and retention decisions to a certain group in the faculty (for example, promotions to full professor by full professors alone) may serve to silence faculty members of lower rank. But the status game may be even more subtle (for example, the unspoken reliance on a faculty clique or informal group for support in decision-making). President Andrew Jackson had his informal advisers, often called his "Kitchen Cabinet." Many administrators or faculty chairmen have an equivalent group of personal advisers. None of these informal status procedures encourages collegial interaction. Attempts to diminish the effects of these procedures have produced some flamboyant, and sometimes useful, procedures.

One "democratic" act has been the elimination of marked parking spaces for administrators. The advertised slogan adopted is, "First come, first served." Another is the calling of a group conference of unit members to resolve a problem of task completion. If the problem is technical, not involving policy or joint procedures, such a meeting may become an exercise in futility. Less common than the group meeting is the employment of an external consultant (often termed a specialist in organizational development) to facilitate collegial interaction. This is based on the twin needs to give overt proof of the endorsement of collegial interaction and to provide a means of administrative withdrawal to facilitate free expression. It is difficult to criticize these open displays of good faith in supporting collegial interaction, but the surest endorsement of the process is persistent development of functional role definitions, the challenge-response dialogue about educational beliefs, and a competent system for the resolution of organizational conflicts.

Conflict Resolution

A belief that conflict can be constructive has been a tenet of democracy. It has led to the adversarial system of seeking justice in British and American court systems. It has been used in electing public officials. Legislatures have based parliamentary systems on it. Academic freedom is justified by it. Both the Magna Carta and the Bill of Rights of the U.S. Constitution declare values of individual liberty to assure man's right to be different and hold different opinions. It is surprising, therefore, to find that it was not until 1926 that the management problem of conflict was addressed in any formal manner—by Mary Parker Follett,[14] and it was twenty-eight years later before Coser published a definitive work on the subject.[15] Still, it is the social systems concept of management which has incorporated it into a conflict resolution system. And the process may be used to cope with assignment conflicts of roles, values, process, behavior, and relations with other units. The dimensions of those conflicts follow:

> Role conflicts are most frequent as (1) misunderstandings among employees sharing a common task, and (2) misunderstandings of other colleagues concerning task assignments.
>
> Process conflicts arise from misunderstandings concerning the details of cooperative effort, for example, timing, methods, and use of common resources.
>
> Behavior conflicts are produced by disappointments with the continued actions of colleagues.
>
> Interunit conflicts are produced by misunderstandings of a unit's role and relations.

Because the work unit is considered a goal-seeking, cooperative enterprise and the unit members are agents for reaching significant subgoals, the conflict resolution system is anchored in a group process.

The work unit is chosen because it has the greatest potential for what Follett called the "integrative" conflict resolution. The potential is quickly identified by an examination of integrative conflict resolution, which can be described by the following steps: (1) achievement of an educational values consensus, and consequently, a common set of goals; (2) identification of employee differences as alternatives for goal accomplishment; (3) choices of alternatives in the light of evidence of probable results; and (4) testing of alternatives chosen. Follett described the alternatives to this type of conflict resolution as (1) dominance, which may have to be exercised by administrative personnel if the integrative process fails or time for its completion exceeds tolerances for task completion, or (2) compromise, which is an expedient to borrow time in major conflicts between groups with nearly equal power. Since integrative resolution depends on attachment to common goals, the work unit provides the site with the most promise. But the manner in which it is used will determine whether the potential is realized.

When the work unit is used as the site of conflict resolution, many procedural questions rise. For example:

> In what group shall it be done (for example, in primary groups, among opinion leaders of primary groups, or among all members of the unit workforce)?
>
> Is an external consultant necessary (for example, a social consultant as described by Sofer,[16] or an intervenor as described by Schmuck and Miles)?[17]
>
> Should the process be standardized by formal rules of procedure and evidence (as in court systems to assure equity, justice, and dispatch)?
>
> Should compliance be enforced by frequent inspection after the decision has been reached?

Options uncovered by responses to these questions reveal a flexibility of reasonable action that may make the system usable in many different kinds of groups.

The group utilized for conflict resolution is carefully chosen to minimize the effort required and maximize the constructive results to be achieved. If role conflicts are merely misunderstandings concerning relative responsibilities in the completion of shared tasks, the group may be restricted to the persons involved. If a primary group, on the other hand, has developed a set of beliefs tangential to, or markedly different from, the consensus of the workforce, the entire work group should be involved because the difference may be the source of constructive development of the organization. If process conflicts affect the entire work group, then it should be the unit of resolution. Behavior conflicts can sometimes be ameliorated by sensitivity (T-Group) orientation procedures to develop collegial expectancy of persistent behavior. Conflict resolution of behavior problems is compassionately restricted to the group affected. Formal grievance procedures are wisely used to protect an employee whose behavior has caused conflict that may lead to termination. Conflicts with other units produce group defensiveness that requires group consideration. The choice of group is, therefore, situational and decided according to the requirements of simplicity and utility.

The decision to use an external consultant cannot be made with any degree of certainty in response to either particular conditions or the choice of a group. If the unit administrator is viewed as a deliberate, fair, objective, goal-oriented, and skillful coordinator, he may occupy the leader's role in conflict resolution more fully than any external consultant. If he is not perceived as that kind of person, another individual in the organization with those characteristics may qualify—at times it may be the personnel director. Of course, if no such person is available in the organization, a concern for constructive results may lead to the choice of an external consultant. In grievance cases requiring formal procedures, it is important to use an experienced arbitrator fully prepared to conduct a formal process.

Formal conflict resolution (usually termed grievance hearings) are used in disputes that may later have to be completed by court action or collective bargaining. At one time, this process was reserved for disputes about the termination of tenured employees. But public policies concerning civil rights, equal pay, equal treatment, and collective bargaining have expanded the list to include (1) discrimination in employment and assignment, (2) equal treatment of women, and (3) interpretation of collective bargaining agreements. Conflicts on these matters are best resolved by formal hearings. The formality may assure equity—or a conviction that equity has been afforded—to the extent that further litigation is considered unnecessary. But excessive use of the formal process may be prompted by undue apprehension concerning further litigation. Every arbitrator has presided over grievance hearings to resolve a conflict that could have been settled in thirty minutes by two persons of good will committed to a common purpose. Constructive benefits of conflict are more often available when the resolution is based on organizational need than on guaranteed rights.

And it is the desire to secure constructive benefits which guides the choice of extent and kind of follow-up of conflict resolution. If the resolution has been formal—and the decision based on legal or contractual obligations—the follow-up must assure full compliance. This usually is a designated administrative task. If the resolution has been a result of group decision—based on common values and evidence, and understood as a more appropriate means of goal accomplishment—it is likely the follow-up is considered a collegial matter and the enforcement (read, group expectancy) is informal. And a persistent reliance by colleagues on agreed performance may be a more powerful motivator than any administrative inspection.

Summary

Each system of management thought has included some rationale and set of procedures for assisting an employee to work effectively in an assignment. The rationales present different views of the employee and his relations to the organization. The procedures differ in ways of motivating, defining roles, securing employee interaction, and resolving conflicts.

The rationale of scientific administration viewed the employee as an entrepreneur whose opportunity for success depended on competition with others to exceed standards of production set by the organization. The human relations system of management thought viewed the employee as a group participant who was directed in his activity by group standards and a group-defined role. The social systems management thought viewed the employee as a goal seeker who shares with others subgoals (tasks) essential to reaching organizational goals.

The differences in rationale prompted differences in recommended procedures. Motivation in scientific administration was economic; in human relations, it was group expectancy; and in social systems, it was a belief (read, an attitude-value constellation) that something should be done. Role definition in scientific administration was the designation of tasks conceived as a block of work necessary to the completion of an organizational plan; in human relations it was a relatively fluid set of tasks based on group recognition of competency; and in social systems it was a set of tasks that were subgoals of the desired organizational goal. Collegial interaction in scientific administration was discouraged unless specified as a part of task completion; the whole system of human relations was based on collegial interaction; and in social systems collegiality was viewed as a means of maintaining a dynamic educational values consensus, developing professional skills, and maintaining professional integrity. Conflict resolution was defined as organizational discipline by scientific administrators; it was considered democratic group action by human relations managers; and it was considered a method of constructive institutional development by social systems administrators.

Notes

1. Frederick W. Taylor, *The Principles of Scientific Management* (New York: Harper and Brothers, 1911; reprint 1942), p. 73.
2. Ibid., p. 95.
3. Ibid., p. 83.
4. Gordon Allport in the "Foreword" to Kurt Lewin, *Resolving Social Conflicts*, Gertrud W. Lewin, ed. (New York: Harper and Brothers, 1948), p. xi.
5. Ibid., p. 59.
6. Ibid., p. 72.
7. Robert Gray Gunderson, "Group Dynamics—Hope or Hoax?" In Warren Bennis, Kenneth Benne, and Robert Chin, eds., *The Planning of Change* (New York: Holt, Rinehart, and Winston, 1961), p. 257.
8. Warren G. Bennis and Herbert A. Shepard, "Group Observation," in *The Planning of Change*, pp. 743-756.
9. H.C. Metcalf and Lionel Urwick, eds., *Dynamic Administration: The Collected Papers of Mary P. Follett* (London: Management Publications Trust, 1941), first paper, entitled "Constructive Conflict."
10. Abraham Maslow, *Motivation and Personality* (New York: Harper and Brothers, 1954).
11. Frederick Herzberg, Bernard Mausner, and Barbara Snyderman, *The Motivation to Work* (New York: John Wiley, 1959).
12. Ibid.
13. Philip Selznick, *Leadership in Administration* (Evanston, Ill.: Row, Peterson, and Company, 1957), p. 150.
14. Metcalf and Urwick, *Papers of Mary P. Follett.*
15. Lewis Coser, *The Social Functions of Conflict* (New York: The Free Press, 1954).
16. Cyril Sofer, *Organizations in Theory and Practice* (New York: Basic Books, 1972), pp. 384-386.
17. Richard A. Schmuck and Matthew B. Miles, eds. *Organization Development in Schools* (Palo Alto, Calif.: National Press Books, 1971), pp. 1-27.

6 Performance Appraisal

Current practices and procedures in the appraisal of educational personnel may be said to be relics of the two systems of administrative thought defined earlier: scientific and human relations management.

Scientific Management Techniques

Essentially, the scientific management approach to evaluation calls for assessing job performance against standards of productivity and efficiency. For all faculty members being evaluated in the public schools, performance standards were established and standardized tests were given to students at the beginning and at the end of the academic year. The results were interpreted as indicators of a teacher's efficiency; gains made by students during the school year were said to show efficiency and productivity. No gain, or minimal progress, meant that the teacher had been ineffective. In many cases where the latter results were found, only the existence of tenure policies or the reluctance of the courts to accept such results as the sole measure of teacher competence prevented the termination or replacement of the teacher. The concept of scientific measurement of teacher effectiveness, nevertheless, was incorporated into the California State Education Code (Section 13487) by the Stull Bill of 1971 (AB 293). The wording shows its scientific evaluation rationale:

> The governing board of each school district shall develop and adopt specific evaluation and assessment guidelines which shall include but not necessarily be limited in content to the following elements,
> (a) The establishment of standards of expected student progress in each area of study and of techniques for the assessment of that progress.
> (b) Assessment of certified personnel competence as it relates to the established standards.
> (c) Assessment of other duties normally required to be performed by certificated employees as an adjunct to their regular assignments.
> (d) The establishment of procedures and techniques for ascertaining that the certificated employee is maintaining a proper control and is preserving a suitable learning environment.[1]

But the establishment of productivity standards as mandated by the Stull Bill proved no more effective than prior practices had been in justifying termination of tenured personnel. Thus the evaluation emphasis was shifted again to the assessments made during the probationary period.

Typically, this process took the form of various kinds of rating schemes, some simplistic, some quite sophisticated. Ratings made by supervisors on a twice-a-year basis may be characterized as simplistic. Using a 0-4 or a tripartite rating scheme of "satisfactory," "unsatisfactory," or "needs improvement," supervisors were often asked to judge such personality traits as loyalty, appearance, voice, honesty, reliability, industry, perserverance, self-reliance, relations with others, and leadership. Although generalized definitions were frequently provided, the ratings were obviously the product of the global judgment of the rater. Other evaluations, added as the result of developments in industrial psychology of the 1920s and 1930s, were intelligence tests, personality surveys, interest inventories, and, most of all, peer group evaluations.[2]

More sophisticated rating schemes developed in recent years have sometimes included straight ranking, alternative ranking, paired comparisons, and forced distributions.[3] Absolute standards ratings sometimes used checklists that featured weighted items. But, whatever the method, all rating systems possessed one common purpose: the identification of the most effective employees in the work group. Because this identification was sought in order to facilitate mangement decisions concerning promotion, termination, and production, it may be said that performance assessment through rating constitutes merely another aspect of the scientific management search for efficiency.

Human Relations Techniques

The human relations approach to administrative thought also produced personnel evaluation schemes. Here the emphasis was on the judgment of colleagues—peer evaluation. In public schools, this type of evaluation was usually confined to selection and promotion committees composed of members of the workforce; it was almost impossible to modify, to any great extent, entrenched scientific administration evaluation schemes designed to test efficiency. Members of selection and promotion committees, ironically, often used ratings of the type described above to express opinions of different candidates.

Of all methods of peer group evaluation, the purest may well be the one generally encountered in colleges and universities. The University of California system offers a prime example; it is also the most elaborate and most expensive. Promotion or termination decisions are initiated by a vote of all departmental faculty members of higher rank than the candidate. The result of this group judgment is referred to a personnel committee composed of representatives of all departments on campus. The personnel committee then seeks the advice of an ad hoc committee, a group composed of professors most likely to be able to evaluate the contributions of the candidate to the university. The ad hoc committee recommendation is then used by the personnel committee to guide its judgment. And, although generally honored, these peer judgments may be overturned by administrative action when exceptional circumstances are cited. Clearly, the complexity of this cumbersome machinery and the great diversity of departments within a large university outmatch the very general criteria provided to all participants in the evaluation process. Thus, in the natural sequence of events —and in an unspoken attempt to stabilize variable departmental interpretations—group compatibility often becomes the true criterion for promotion or termination.

There are other, more far-reaching problems resulting from peer conformity types of evaluation. Indeed, it would seem that the employee's adaptation to group demands is given prime attention. Such characteristics as the candidate's concept of collegiality, personal goal accomplishment within the parameters of organizational goals, self-motivation, professional identification, and the employee's membership in other types of social organizations are largely ignored. In short, group conformity demands bid fair to be as stultifying as scientific administration demands for efficiency in restricting the creativity of the employee. If the creative potential of each employee is to be considered a valuable resource for the development of the organization, it would seem prudent to seek a system of personnel evaluation that will free it for use. In this context, it may be useful to discuss some of the ideas of social systems administration.

Social Systems Evaluation Policies

There are at least six categories of assessment policies that constitute the component parts of a reasonably comprehensive examination of teacher competence. These are:

1. Role Fulfillment

Although it may be assumed that assignment procedures have provided each employee with a role to fill in the workforce, roles can only be defined under the following conditions: (1) if the assigned tasks are described, (2) if the acceptable skills needed for their completion are delineated, and (3) if their normal sequences of development are formulated. If these conditions have been met, evaluation procedures can be used to identify (1) the skills possessed, (2) the order of appropriate skills to learn next, and (3) the most effective learning procedures to become proficient in those skills.

2. Reinforcement

A particularly productive aspect of the evaluation process is to use it as a way to assist the employee in developing confidence in his performance. Of course, all skill-requiring activities are not immediately confirmed as successful by the results achieved. This is particularly true of the education profession. In effect, there are times in teaching when the only confirmation of success comes from the assurance given by a colleague that the skill is indeed displayed and that it is fully in accord with the state of the art. But in all work group situations, when the skills used are inappropriate, or only partly effective, the employee needs to know this before he can improve his performance. Thus it would seem reasonable to suggest that reinforcement be made proximate to the display of the skill, both in time and place. And evaluation should be made a continuous process, not a scheduled once- or twice-a-year event.

3. Professional Evaluation

This category of assessment within the evaluation process is universally desirable, no more and no less for the educational systems than for all other organizations. Reinforcement, as defined in number 2 above, will lead to self-confidence only if the person providing it is known to represent the profession faithfully and accurately. Indeed, an encouraging or supportive colleague, who is a respected professional and himself possesses the required skills, may well inspire enough confidence to meet reinforcement requirements.

4. Collegiality

This is an element of the evaluation process not always understood for its full impact. Collegiality consists of mutual assistance in skill development; it requires a commitment to its principles by everyone in the workforce. The administrative commitment may prompt support by policies of providing substitutes for colleagues assisting each other, or the recruitment of colleagues from other work units to assist. There are other manifestations of collegiality that can occur within the school system: visits to other classrooms, for example, where specific teaching strategies may be observed, or experimentation with a broad spectrum of students in other classrooms. Whatever the method, collegiality is likely to result in examination and agreement among the members of the workforce as to what constitutes desirable aspects of skilled behavior.

5. Creativity

Agreement on desirable skills may tend to exclude another important dimension of professional behavior, notably, creativity. There are in the educational profession, as elsewhere, a number of people who have unique backgrounds or unique capabilities. They may complete tasks in unorthodox ways or obtain strong results in an individual fashion. This capacity should not only be discouraged; it should be given professional reinforcement with due consideration of results achieved.

6. Self-Evaluation

It would seem that at this point all elements knit into a clearly defined entity. Indeed, the ultimate goal of an evaluative process that functions well is the development of a sophisticated professional, capable of self-evaluation. This condition may be the millennium, and never reached, principally because skills deteriorate or become obsolete, or more likely because new skills are continuously needed for meeting new task requirements. However, it would appear that as time goes on and situations become more familiar, the employee develops the capability of recognizing his own errors as he goes about his tasks. This desirable state of affairs does not, in any way, proscribe the need for collegiality. It does translate to mean that the burden of mutual assistance may be eased as situations tend to stabilize and become more routine.

Thus the intent of the six evaluation policies just described is to achieve a balanced perspective of what is required to obtain a measure of teacher competence. Acceptance and implementation of these policies, then, requires the development of procedures compatible with this intent. Such procedural adaptations, although markedly different from current practice, are necessary in order to establish a pattern of employee evaluation compatible with utilizing to the fullest the unique creative potential of each employee.

Social Systems Evaluation Procedures

If the intent of the evaluation process is to reinforce desirable employee behavior and build professional confidence, four specific areas of procedure should be taken into consideration. These are:

1. The Timing of Evaluation

Educational evaluations, as mentioned earlier, should be carried out proximate to the display of the skills. As the for time element, Flanagan explored a series of cues that should be heeded. He defined cues as a joint recognition by the employee and the supervisor that "critical incidents" of performance were apparent.[4] Following Flanagan's idea, three such categories are identifiable: (1) personal, (2) organization, and (3) community. In school systems cues may appear when the employee encounters difficulties in mastering skills, when he tries to coordinate his work with others, and when he tries to coordinate his work with nonschool educational agencies. The three categories may be examined within this context.

Personal Cues. It may be recalled that the social systems type of evaluation rests on the assumptions that the skills required are known to the employee, that these skills have been defined either during the selection process or during prior evaluations, and that the employee is motivated to learn all the skills involved. Logically, then, the employee's inability to master the required skills provides a cue to him to seek evaluative services.

Organization Cues. These are often reflective of personal cues, if on a broader canvas. If an inability to learn skills required for the effective functioning of the organization persists, despite the provision of evaluative and coaching assistance, further evaluation may be indicated. For example, formal as well as informal evaluations of teachers by students may offer a cue to prompt evaluation. A word of caution is in order about student evaluations. the temptation to treat student opinions of faculty as comprehensive evaluations should be resisted. Although student opinions do serve as one type of cue, the dangers of overestimating their value has been reported by Aleamoni and Sheehan.[5]

Other organizational cues are provided by colleagues who recognize the inability of the work group to fulfill its complete role. This type of cue is extremely valuable, particularly because the success of a cooperative enterprise (a school system) depends on the definition, assignment, and completion of cooperative duties.

Community Cues. Cues may be provided also by individuals in community institutions with which the educational organization must cooperate in order to achieve educational goals. For example, a group of parents who agree on the members' disappointment or disapproval of a particular teacher or other school employee provides a powerful incentive for evaluation. Other examples are (1) a probation officer displaying asperity and protesting about the lack of cooperation by a school employee, or (2) the complaints of a community employer who has been supporting a work-study program. It is evident that a school employee about whom community complaints are being registered will want to cooperate, not only because of a professional obligation, but also because he wishes to be defended.

Thus the Flanagan concept of "critical incidents" is a viable one and should aid in deciding when to conduct an evaluation. The process, however, should NOT be initiated without giving careful consideration to the characteristics of the person who is to do the evaluation.

2. *The Selection of Evaluators*

Because confidence in the evaluator by the individual being evaluated is germane to reinforcement, the selection of the evaluator should involve consideration of (1) compatibility and (2) skills possessed by the evaluator.

Compatibility. Compatibility is probably best fostered by allowing a choice of evaluators. If several individuals have been identified as skilled evaluators within the unit workforce, the employee's choice is likely to be guided by his own sense of who, among the corps of people available, offers compatibility. The selected evaluator can then be made available by the provision of substitutes for the evaluation period or by rearranging his schedule of work to free him for the service.

Skills. Selection of skilled evaluators is complicated by the current professional status of educational practice. This problem was explored by Broudy, as follows:

> Unlike the new plumber or carpenter, the new teacher cannot take counsel with an older practitioner and be confident of receiving help. Because the older practitioners do not share a consensus on proper procedures, their individual experience may or may not be applicable to the novice in distress.[6]

Further, Broudy ruled out turning to professors of education for solid advice on procedures:

> As for professors of education, it is difficult to find many who are both nationally known and whose allegiance to some school, some project, some professional coterie does not impair their credibility.[7]

If Broudy's caveats are valid—and they appear to be true reflections of a complex situation in the school systems—what would be required to put together a corps of evaluators? At least two criteria should predominate: evaluators should be able to (1) relate procedures to tasks assigned and (2) justify them by systematic analysis within a conceptual framework (that is, they should be able to justify their skill analyses as the most appropriate means of achieving educational goals). Although this type of evaluator may, as a result, appear to provide only a provincial view of the profession, he does serve as a means of selecting a course of action, and, furthermore, satisfying the employee's need for assistance.

These procedures do seem to be somewhat more time consuming than evaluation practices now used in public schools. But the "coaching" technique which they involve does present a method of achieving reinforcement of desired behavior that comprises less opportunity for error or failure.

3. The Evaluation Process

In most instances, the reinforcement of desired behavior concerns itself with a focused examination of a single skill, or a group of skills—those that are integral to the completion of an assigned task. As described earlier, there are a number of cues within areas of school personnel assingments that point quite clearly to the appropriate skill, or skills, to be examined.

In addition, reinforcement cannot be assured unless the evaluator has full information about the procedures being used, including those that were tried and rejected, and some evidence of the degree of success achieved by the use of each. The gathering of this information requires (1) joint probing to determine the existence of previous practices, (2) joint examination of such practices, (3) relevant data within the employee's or the organization's records, and (4) observation of the employee at work. What this accomplishes, once the data are in hand, is the possibility of comparing present procedures to the procedures that proved successful for task completion under the same or similar role assignments within the organization. Comparisons between current practices and known, acceptable ones may lead to several types of reinforcement. First of all, the employee, on occasion, can be assured that he is using the most appropriate procedures the organization has identified as being successful. Or the reinforcement may prove to be partial: earlier procedures are found to have been useful in part, but need to be amended according to district experience. In this case the evaluator should assist the employee to experiment with different procedures until together they achieve the ends sought. In other instances the evaluator may reinforce the employee by noting that, although few of the procedures conform to district experience, they serve effectively for task completion because the pattern of procedures unique to the organization, are nonetheless well suited to the unusual skill of the employee. Each of these types of reinforcement provides assurance to the employee that he can use the skills displayed with confidence, and that they contribute to the accomplishment of organizational goals.

These practices may be critized as being (1) informal, (2) a continuing process that constitutes a part of supervision, or (3) an activity that offers little to aid personnel planning, accountability, or termination of the incompetent. And these criticisms may be justified if the results of evaluations are not incorporated into evaluation reports.

4. Evaluation Reports

It is self-evident that the ability of an educational unit to perform is determined by the skill potential of the employees assigned to it. The maintenance or expansion of unit capability may require the termination or replacement of an employee incapable of mastering required skills, or incapable of mastering them within the time constraints of the unit. It may require the transfer to other duties of an employee whose skills cannot be utilized within the unit. It surely requires the steady, effective reinforcement of desirable skills displayed by unit employees. Thus evaluation reports become a necessity if the unit is to accomplish its purposes.

An evaluator's report should identify with clarity the skills possessed by the person being evaluated. If skills are only partly mastered, the report should give some estimate of the time required for their mastery. If the skills confirmed in evaluation are inappropriate to the assignment, the report should indicate the alternate assignments for which they might be essential. The report should be made not only to the unit supervisor, but to the personnel department which maintains the skills inventory essential to organizational planning, institutes procedures for transfer, and cooperates in termination.

The evaluation policies and procedures described above present a consistent pattern of employee performance appraisal intended to maximize the organization's ability to utilize the creative potential of the staff. But consistency and logic are seldom sufficient to overcome the inertia resulting from custom, tradition, and habit. Indeed, there are a number of obstacles that must be recognized and overcome if the described policies and procedures of evaluation are to be instituted.

Obstacles to Adoption

Obstacle No. 1: Diversity of Educational Practice

As noted earlier, there exists little agreement in the educational profession concerning appropriate procedures for the completion of educational tasks. Recall Broudy's pessimistic view:

> There is virtually no consensus on procedures such as are found in carpentry, plumbing, law, medicine, accounting, or architecture. On the contrary, the more idiosyncratically a teacher behaves, the more likely is he or she to be praised as innovative, imaginative, or ingenious.[8]

Perhaps this unfortunate state of affairs is to be expected in an endeavor that must cope with an infinite number of learning problems of an almost endless variety of individuals. Sometimes the task would seem almost beyond the limits of experimental confirmation of rational practices. And the reasoned theories, the recommended practices, and the generally narrow-scope investigations of educational problems are almost as endless. At the same time, it must be recognized that the profession itself has not shown the disposition to arrive at some consensus of practice it can recommend to its members. This failure to solve a thorny problem would seem to make the profession an unreliable source to provide guidance for preparatory programs and school district practice. Under these circumstances, the school district is obliged to carve out for itself an operational definition of approved procedures.

The district is obliged to develop procedures that can be used with confidence by members of the staff. This requires a determination of goals, tasks, and roles within the educational beliefs of the workforce. Students' and staff members' tasks and roles should be defined with the same clarity as the system's goals. Procedures should be endorsed to the extent that they assist all participants in fulfilling their roles by completing their assigned tasks. This kind of operational validation, of course, requires an expenditure of staff effort for inquiry—an effort that has not been characteristic of school districts to date. The acceptance of this responsibility by a school district, however, would aid not only in making evaluation constructive, but would serve to come to terms with the meaning of another obstacle: accountability.

Obstacle No. 2: Accountability

Essentially, accountability responds to an understandable demand for educational employees to accomplish something by their work—and to give others an idea of what was accomplished. Most often, indeed ever since it burst on the national consciousness, accountability has been interpreted in terms borrowed from the efficiency-productivity concepts of the scientific approach to administration. It asked, and still asks, among other things, for teachers to produce gains as measured by the difference between students' pre- and posttest scores on standardized achievement tests. Not only have many states mandated the use of testing for these purposes, but a large number of federal grants earmarked for elementary and secondary education were contingent on evaluation—requirements that were met by school districts with the imposition of various kinds of tests. As time went on, some of these tests became more and more sophisticated. For example, during the past decade, many educators placed their trust in criterion-referenced tests. Although diagnostic in nature, such tests did not substantially alter the commitment to personnel evaluation based on the examination of student test results. So it was with the much-discussed, fairly new Competency- (Professionally) Based Teacher Evaluation system, which makes an attempt at producing a more usable (read, reflective of specific skill domains) system of personnel evaluation. But when one examines these tests closely, it becomes apparent that they are not sufficient to reflect the many things a teacher should be able to do. What is needed here is what was needed before: a consensus on procedures. So many types of competency lists were drawn up that their proliferation made any individual listing virtually unusable in any given evaluation situation.

It may be argued that most accountability systems now in operation within districts have three features in common. They fail to confront three different, if crucial, problems. They sidestep (1) the lack of agreement on educational goals, (2) the almost unbelievable diversity of students in classrooms, and (3) the failure of the teaching profession to endorse practices of known value in coping with the learning problems of different students. Considering these points, it hardly seems surprising that accountability does not work. *An educational employee cannot be expected to produce uniform results with diverse students when what is to be produced is uncertain and the procedures to produce them are in dispute.*

But the need for all parties to obtain a proper balance among conflicting needs, rights, and demands would indicate that a different definition of educational accountability must be found. To find such a definition, perhaps the time has come for education to borrow from other professions. The language used by the courts in determining professional malpractice by doctors of medicine or lawyers is couched in terms of responsibility rather than fluctuating, arbitrarily imposed standards. The courts have ruled that malpractice is not proved if doctors or lawyers "exercise good judgment . . . due care and diligence . . . perform as a reasonably prudent and carefully trained person . . . use requisite skill. . . ."[9] At the risk of sounding dramatic, it should be remembered that these words concern those who deal with an individual's legal rights, and in some instances with life itself. It would seem, therefore, that Johnson's position urging a similarly mature approach in evaluating educational personnel is entirely reasonable. Johnson referred to the need to examine "the intents teachers form and the consequent acts teachers take."[10] This description points up the need for school districts to spend the time in developing procedures they are willing to endorse so that some sort of consensus can finally be reached. But even if all these desirable events come to pass—and acceptable standards are agreed upon—the district must still be willing to take into account the possibility that a teacher may NOT secure an observable change in the performance of a group of students. There are a number of reasons why this might occur: perhaps the students were placed in an incorrect instructional group, or the goals sought were inappropriate for their level of accomplishment, or the context of the instruction could not foster learning. Maybe, too, the art itself was deficient.

But, if and when accountability is firmly anchored upon professional endorsement, there are still other obstacles that must be considered. Among these is the influence of the working group upon each individual participant.

Obstacle No. 3: Group Influences on Employee Behavior

Sofer's description of group influences seems particularly apt in this context:

> Interaction between and within the work groups in the organization will be infused with emotions. . . . No work group will keep consistently to its task. Each will alternate instead between manifest tasks and what would appear from outside to be emotional interferences with the real work. However described by the members, the sources of this interference will be largely in their own interaction, including the hopes and disappointments of members concerning each other.[11]

What this really means it that evaluation, of whatever nature, is unlikely to be confined to a formal process alone. Evaluations are made by everyone—students, colleagues, parents, community individuals interested in schools, acquaintances. Although informal and unstructured, these assessments must be handled carefully. They are aimed in a number of directions, some to the attention of the employee, and some, no less emotionally, to other individuals in the organization. But whatever the communication technique, gratuitous evaluations eventually reach the ears of the employee. Within the employee, they prompt defensive reactions and, sometimes, modifications of behavior. If the organization, for its part, is unable or unprepared to cope with unstructured assessments, the rationality of the formal process may degenerate into irrational behavior, both by the employee and the organization. It is, therefore, important that all concerned anticipate the interference of emotional assessments; indeed, part of the recommended evaluation process is designed to cope with its effects.

A productive method of handling gratuitous evaluations is to treat them as cues to prompt more formal and rigorous evaluations. For one thing, the employee deserves to be defended when he becomes the object of criticism. The organization should seek out valid and reliable evidence from the formal evaluation process and examine the worth of emotional assessments within that context. But it must be remembered that the employee must be given fair treatment; gratuitous assessments should, therefore, never be taken as more than cues. Yet it is also obvious that an organization cannot initiate a formal investigation each time someone makes a comment about an employee. It would seem, then, that the most effective way of dealing with this kind of situation is to adopt some techniques that will minimize the opportunity for gratuitous criticism.

One technique is the use of the assignment procedures suggested in the preceding chapter on assignment and transfer. By clarifying roles, by resolving conflicts that arise from assignments, and by suggesting the quality and potentiality of interaction the entire staff can develop a more sophisticated expectancy of the behavior of each workforce member. It is probably safe to say that if this process were used with community groups, board-administrator personnel, district administrators, and in school attendance area role clarification some emotional evaluations that affect relations between work group members, between school and community, and between administrators and boards of trustees may be minimized.

Another technique involves the sensitivity training group, which is probably more effective when used as an orientation process among members of a working group. These groups are generally formed in order to provide each member with some information concerning the characteristic reactions of participants to many types of group situations. This foreknowledge allows the luxury of avoiding emotional reactions because it affords the ability to refrain from establishing (or provoking or emphasizing) a situation that would generate such reactions. It requires no deep psychological insight or expertise to realize that knowing how an individual characteristically reacts to a recurring situation minimizes the emotional reaction to it when it occurs. It is generally surprise—or being taken unaware—that provokes emotional, spontaneous reactions. Such foreknowledge may also serve to encourage colleagues to make criticisms to the individual concerned rather than, under the influence of an emotional response, to some other person.

But any procedure adopted to minimize gratuitous evaluations is sure to do no more than reduce the number; it will never eliminate them. The best protection of an employee against evaluations is his self-confidence in his own procedures and reactions. It is self-assurance that must be fostered. Effective evaluation procedures in their role of reinforcing behavior can provide self-confidence. But this prime purpose of evaluation is constantly being jeopardized by one more obstacle: employees' persistent tendencies to orient all evaluation procedures to dismissal.

Obstacle No. 4: Dismissal Evaluation

There are, without doubt, countless employees who view evaluation as a formal procedure that legitimates dismissal. Indeed, the association of evaluation with termination may be fostered by the practice of conducting evaluations frequently during probationary service—and seldom thereafter. In addition, evaluations intended to reinforce desirable behavior have frequently been nonspecific concerning the behavior to be endorsed. As a result, reinforcement appraisal is often greeted by the employee with skepticism. Or, as Schulz's comic strip would have it, when cautioned by Charlie Brown to congratulate the members of the baseball team which had just beaten them, Lucy called out to other members, "Come on, team. It's hypocrite time."[12]

It may not be possible to eliminate all of the evaluation apprehension of the probationer. In fact, it may not be desirable to eliminate it entirely among permanent employees. There are instances where termination after evaluation is necessary, or better, for both the employee and the organization. But undue apprehension can be reduced by (1) maintaining a persistent emphasis during the process on reinforcement of desirable behavior, (2) applying insightful emphasis on the manner in which absent skills can be learned, and (3) putting what causes terminations into the proper perspective. If the employee knows that no such action is contemplated until and unless every effort has been made to assist him in developing appropriate skills—and a conclusion has been reached either that the skills cannot be learned, or the time of learning exceeds organizational requirements—the organization can use evaluations as the best antidote for undue dismissal apprehension and turn the process into a positive activity.

Summary

The prime purpose of performance appraisal is the reinforcement of productive professional behavior—the development of confident, skilled effort in the completion of assigned tasks. If this purpose is to be served, appropriate evaluation policies should demonstrate an intent to

Facilitate role fulfillment.

Reinforce desirable professional behavior.

Emphasize professionally recognized procedures.

Utilize colleagues in the evaluation process.

Develop the employee's capacity for self-evaluation.

Procedures growing from these policies would:

Time evaluations so they occur proximate to the display of the behavior to be examined.

Select evaluators best qualified to be able to reinforce desirable behavior.

Direct attention in each evaluation episode to a single skill, or unified group of skills.

Utilize the evaluation reports skillfully to promote, terminate, transfer, or develop the employee's potential.

The adoption of this type of performance appraisal system may be contingent on recognition and removal of the following obstacles:

The lack of professional consensus concerning goals and procedures of education.

Accountability defined in terms of productivity and efficiency.

Reluctance to cope with the organizational effects of gratuitous evaluations.

Organizational emphasis on evaluation for termination.

Notes

1. California *Education Code*, ch. 361, article 5.5 (1978) sections 13485-13487.
2. Cyril Sofer, *Organizations in Theory and Practice* (New York: Basic Books, 1972), pp. 43-62.
3. Craig E. Schneier and Richard W. Beatty, *Personnel Administration Today* (Menlo Park, Calif.: Addison-Wesley, 1978), pp. 297-304.
4. John C. Flanagan, "A New Approach to Evaluating Personnel," *Personnel* 26 (1949):35-42.
5. Lawrence M. Aleamoni and Daniel S. Sheehan, "On the Invalidity of Student Ratings for Administration of Personnel Decisions," *Journal of Higher Education* 47 (1976):607-611.
6. Harry S. Broudy, "The Fiduciary Basis of Education: A Crisis in Credibility," *Phi Delta Kappan* 59 (1978):88. © 1978 by Phi Delta Kappa, Inc., Reprinted with permission.

7. Ibid. Reprinted with permission.

8. Ibid. Reprinted with permission.

9. John W. Wade, "The Attorney's Liability for Negligence," *Professional Negligence* (Nashville, Tenn.: Williams Printing Company, 1960), p. 224; Ted M. Warshafsky, "Approaches to Hospital Negligence," *Case and Comment* 5 (1960):12.

10. Henry C. Johnson, Jr., "Court, Craft, and Competence: A Reexamination of Teacher Evaluation Procedures," *Phi Delta Kappan* 57 (1976):606-611.

11. Sofer, *Organizations*, p. 227.

12. Charles Schulz, "Peanuts," *Los Angeles Times*, November 14, 1977.

7 Human Resource Development

A major component of personnel administration is personnel development; every system of administrative thought has included its own recommended procedures to achieve employee personal and professional growth. But each recommendation, like the system that spawned it, was shaped by the social, political, and economic forces of its time and place.

In scientific administration, the view of the employee as an entrepreneur logically placed the assignment of the responsibility for development on the employee himself. In school administration, this attitude was translated into merit (in essence automatic) increases when credits were earned in colleges and universities, or in inservice courses made available by the employer. Generally, the school systems did not subsidize this activity (save for column advances in the salary schedule); the cost was borne by the employee.

The employee also selected what he wanted to study, often without (or with minimal) advice from the employer. Indeed, the school system abstained from either directing or unquestioningly utilizing his new skills and knowledge. If, for example, he chose to study administration, and if there were beginning administrative positions, he had to compete with others in and out of the system to gain appointment. This policy of individual freedom of choice and action was consistent with a rapidly expanding economy which was based on liassez-faire thinking and which drew much of its workforce from either rural or foreign populations. Thus administrators placed prime emphasis on efficiency and competitiveness, the twin tenets of the scientific approach. But unregulated competition generated problems that undermined the soundness of the democratic system as a whole (exploitation of natural and human resources, political manipulation by Tammany Hall in New York City and other similar groups, special economic and political privileges achieved by selfish economic interests, and so on). In an attempt to correct these excesses and institute more balanced practices, the human relations approach to administrative thought captured the attention of both business and educational leaders.

In human relations, the employee was viewed as a full participant in the democratic group. An earlier chapter described the watchwords of this kind of administrative thought as "group maintenance" and "group dynamics." Personnel development, here, meant finding and expanding a suitable role for the employee within the working group, a process termed "fusion," by Dwight Bakke.[1] In schools, development of personnel was seen as self-fulfillment and was interpreted in terms of psychosocial needs. Open discussions were held in faculty meetings; vertical, horizontal, administrative, and ad hoc committees were formed; task forces were created; cooperative "action" research was sponsored; faculty socials and picnics were scheduled; bowling, tennis, and golfing competition among staff members was encouraged; sensitivity training was developed; and teachers were encouraged to place great emphasis on the psychosocial needs of their students. These concepts of personnel development were consistent with the transformation of a laissez-faire economy into a "mixed" economy shared by private investors and the public, the development of administrative controls by both state and federal governments, and the development of voluntary and governmental cooperation in the relief of unfortunates in the society. But the preccupation with self-fulfillment in a group proved to have two serious weaknesses: (1) it fostered an atomistic, fragmented society, in which differences between selfishly interested groups led to conflicts too numerous to resolve promptly, and (2) it caused neglect of purposes that groups have in common. And unresponsiveness to societal requirements beyond individual psychosocial needs led to experimentation in personnel development in a social systems context.

It may be said that, in social systems administrative thought, personnel are considered a form of capital assets. Development of the employee will (1) add to the ability of an organization to achieve its objectives and (2) offset the cost of the development program by expected increases in productivity. Because each employee is viewed as a goal seeker, the organization has to develop policies and procedures that will enable the employee to achieve goals which he perceives as valuable. To achieve this end, the organization should do the following:

1. Clarify organizational goals and component subgoals.
2. Develop organizational participation in terms of joint achievement of subgoals to realize organizational ends.
3. Assist employees to develop the skills essential to goal accomplishment.
4. Reinforce desirable employee behavior.

These practices are required in a technologically oriented, metropolitan society in which each individual is a member of many groups, every organization is, in part, dependent for its success on the cooperation of many other organizations, and political processes emphasize the importance of the individual. This concept of human resource development is, indeed, reflective of today's society. Its adoption by school systems, however, requires substantial changes in current administrative and personnel procedures now largely oriented to a mix of scientific and human relations administrative practices.

The most urgent—and probably the most complex—of the needed procedures may prove to be the determination of goals and subgoals precisely enough to assign coherent and valued subgoals to individuals as tasks to be completed.

Clarification of Organizational Goals and Subgoals

For school systems, goal determination precise enough, and practical enough, to lead to assignment of subgoals as tasks is a complex endeavor. This is not only because of the wide diversity of students in metropolitan school classes, but because of the multiplicity of institutions that compete for the learning time of children and youth. The list of places and activities that demand attention boggles the mind. It may include, among others, radio, television, musical events, museum activities, the family, a church, Boy Scouts, Girl Scouts, Campfire, Little League, Pop Warner football, John Wooden basketball, the library, magazines, newspapers, the neighborhood gang, a local employer, the juvenile court, a fraternity or sorority, an interest club, a dramatics society, or a political party. Even if it were possible to arrive at a reliable educational values consensus, and thereby assure a set of tenable goals for the community educational program, the role of each institution in the community program would still have to be defined to facilitate their cooperation with each other and the school system. Unfortunately, the procedures to arrive at role definition have not been agreed upon or firmly drawn, but at least one plan has been developed.

The plan was incorporated into a manual prepared by Robert Melcher and intended for use in eleven school districts of the state of Washington in 1974 and 1975 by the Washington State Department of Instruction. Procedures for defining the roles of various institutions in the community educational program were based on linear charting techniques designed by Hijams and Bern,[2] It was expected that Melcher's decision descriptions would be interpreted as follows:

> General Responsibility: The community agency guides and directs the completion of tasks through the agency delegated to hold operating responsibility;

Operating Responsibility: The agency is directly responsible for the execution of the task;

Specific Responsibility: The agency completes the tasks;

Must be Consulted: The agency, if the decision affects its work, must be called upon before any decision is made, or approval is granted, to render advice or relate information, but not to make the decision nor grant approval;

May be Consulted: The agency may be called upon to relate information, render service, or make recommendations;

Must be Notified: The agency must be notified of action that has been taken;

Must Approve: The agency (other than those holding general and operating responsibility) must approve or disapprove.[3]

It was anticipated that these role decisions would be reached in a group format including representatives of all agencies. This would serve not only the role definition process, but facilitate the resolution of conflicts. But it was expected that the group process would be more effective if certain problems could be anticipated.

The anticipated problems in the community educational role definition process were as follows:

A strong educational values consensus would facilitate the process.

Representatives of community institutions were more likely to secure cooperation of their associates if they were policy leaders.

The school may be asked, too often, to fulfill a supervisory (general responsibility) role.

The needs for nonschool agencies—not in existence now—might be discovered.

Duplications of educational effort would be discovered.

Maintenance of coordinated effort might tax school resources.

Even though Project Interaction—as the manual and experiment were entitled—was conducted by consultants trained by Melcher's Mangement Responsibility Guidance Corporation, the prime concern was development of administrative techniques. There is little evidence, as a result, of the success of the proposed role identification procedure for community educational agencies. The possibility, however, of arriving at such a coordinated plan constitutes merely a first step in the goal development program. Within the confines of its community educational role, the school system must move forward and define, as well, the roles of each of its units or it cannot mount an orderly program of goal development.

After unit goals have been defined, the final step requires allocating tasks to individuals within the unit. The charting procedure recommended by Melcher may prove useful to this process, as shown in figure 7-1.

Despite the seemingly logical, straightforward utility of the successive steps of goal allocation (that is, defining the community educational role of schools, the role of different school units, and the role of each individual in goal achievement), it is fraught with conflict. One such conflict was pointed out by Lawrence and Lorsch, who identified conflicts between units as the product of disparity of duties assigned to each.[4] Sofer suggested that units develop defensiveness, as follows:

> Each department or division in an organization, with its unique tasks and responsibilities, tends to interpret any new idea, technical or administrative, in terms of its potential impact on the well-being of its members.[5]

There is no question that some conflicts are intrinsic to the fulfillment of traditional roles. For example, skills such as reading and writing require constant attention in each of the thirteen or more years of schooling; yet the elementary grades (K-8) generally concentrate on skills and attitudes, while secondary schools (9-12) emphasize the acquisition of knowledge. It would seem evident that nothing less than a strong educational values consensus will lessen the impact of conflict or make its resolution a possibility.

And there are other factors that add to the extent of conflict. Major among these is the wide diversity of our society, which, by virtue of environment and milieu, tends to complicate the problem of securing cooperation among community agencies. One school, for an example, may be surrounded by an educational wasteland; another may exist in a neighborhood full of libraries, interested parents, active churches, successful youth programs, and talented citizens. The goals of these two schools are necessarily different. One school may be staffed with experienced, productive, mature personnel; another may be staffed by beginners—a condition contrary to good personnel practice, but sometimes unavoidable. Goals in these two schools are different because of staff potential. Yet each unit's role must be defined in terms of tasks to be completed and goals to be achieved.

It would appear, then, that not until a procedure for resolving role conflicts has been established can cooperative action be facilitated. Role definition, whether in the community, the school system itself, or among working members of a unit, should be accomplished within a conflict resolution milieu to be successful.

TASK DESCRIPTOR / POSITION/ORGANIZATION	Principal	Asst. Principal I	Asst. Principal II	Head Counselor	Dept Chairman	Student Activ. Dir.	Media Center Dir.	Board of Ed.	Superintendent	Ed. Services	Bus. Services	Teacher	Student	Parent	PTA
Develop instructional & curricular plans & programs & determine steps required to achieve them.	A C D	B	C D	C D	C D	C D	C D	G	G	C D	F	C D	C F	E F	
Formulate co-curricular plans & programs to meet developmental needs of students.	A C G	C D	C D	C D	E F	B			E	C D	C F	C	C D	C F	C D
Develop schedules & content of student, parent, teacher &/or counselor conferences.	C	A C D	C D	B	C F	C F	C F			E		C D	E F	E F	
Establish school goals, objectives & priorities based on identified needs of students & community.	A B	C D	C D	C D	C D	C D	C D	E F	C G	C F	C F	C D	C D	C F	C F
Evaluate content & relevancy of specific courses, compare results with commitment & take corrective action, if required.	A F	C D	B	C D	C D	E			E F	C D		C D	C	C	

A GENERAL RESPONSIBILITY
B OPERATING RESPONSIBILITY
C SPECIFIC RESPONSIBILITY
D MUST BE CONSULTED
E MAY BE CONSULTED
F MUST BE NOTIFIED
G MUST APPROVE

Figure 7-1. Role Definitions: Management Responsibility Guide

Briefly reviewed, goal development and clarification is necessary to give the employee an opportunity to work on tasks valued by him in a work unit staffed by colleagues whose assignments complement his, and whose joint effort with him produces a result of which all can be proud.

The successful incorporation of processes that achieve this desirable end may facilitate the development of another human resource goal: full participation of the employee in the work of the organization.

Development of Organizational Participation

In human resource development, the term participation describes the creation or existence of an organizational climate in which it is possible for each employee to contribute maximally to the determination of goals, assignments of responsibility, determination of methods, control of quality, and the maintenance of the organization. Procedures for achieving this desirable state of affairs, to the benefit of both the organization and the employee, are not the same in European and American practice. It may be useful here to comment briefly on the perception of organizational participation as it is carried out in some European countries before describing the American perception of what it entails.

Actually, in Europe the system is termed codetermination. It may be argued that the prefix denotes a joint effort of equal magnitude by the workforce and management. This appears to be the case, because a key feature is the installation of labor representatives on boards of directors. The concept has become prevalent throughout much of Europe and was approved by the Common Market countries. An illustration is the Swedish Act on Employee Participation in Decision Making, which became effective on January 1, 1977. This act is representative of the European concept because, as Logue suggested, (1) it modified management rights to "direct and allocate work"; (2) it barred managerial secrecy; (3) it mandated employee participation in decision-making; and (4) it neutralized management's traditional legal representation advantage in labor courts.[6] Logue also suggested that it represented but the most recent step in a series of laws enacted to fulfill the same trinity of purposes: (1) to strengthen the power of shop and safety stewards; (2) to reduce the power of management to terminate employees; and (3) to provide for employee representation on boards of directors. The significance of the Scandinavian model of participation was interpreted by McIsaac as follows:

> The fact is that job rights and, in particular, an individual's right to secure employment and stable income are being elevated to political and legal parity with property rights, notably including rights of investors.[7]

Logue noted that the Swedish procedure was created at the insistence of labor unions, a force whose membership includes some 75 percent of wage and salary employees. Furthermore, Logue pointed out that the unions were in control of the Social Democratic party, which, until recently, had been the party in power for as long as a generation. Thus, to summarize, organizational participation in Europe is a formal movement, government dictated, and raises employees' rights to a par with managers' and investors' rights.

These procedures do not parallel American practices for securing employee participation. Of course, our demographics are different; in the United States, union membership consists of somewhat less than 25 percent of the wage and salary employees of the country (23.8 percent).[8] And we have no labor party. Our union leaders view codetermination as a continuation of the traditional labor policy of relying on collective bargaining under government rules to achieve economic ends. Batt and Weinberg quoted Thomas Donohue, executive assistant to George Meany, Head of the AFL-CIO, on the union position, as follows: "We do not seek to be a partner in management—co-determination offers little to American unions in the performance of their job unionism role."[9]

Thus full participation in the United States is left to a consistent set of administrative practices aimed at producing what was described as organizational climate at the beginning of this section.

There are several interpretations of what constitutes an organizational climate conducive to employee participation. Likert described twenty-four characteristics, which can be summarized as follows:

> There are common goals and they are derived from a values consensus produced by joint effort;
>
> Collegial roles have been clearly defined so that cooperation within the organization is supportive, mutual, and serviced by an effective communication system;
>
> Participants in the organization, including administrators, influence each other;
>
> Role definitions are clear enough to allow each participant to make decisions freely and without too much restraint;
>
> Creativity and determination produce a willingness to resolve problems often considered "impossible";

Despite the level of consensus, common action is possible on significant group problems; and

Members of the group trust each other.[10]

Miles's descriptive definitions can be stated more succinctly. He specified characteristics of organizational climate as follows:

Goals are in focus;

Communication is adequate;

All resources are used effectively;

Power is equalized;

Work satisfies the participants;

Creativity is displayed by individuals and the group;

The organization is responsive positively and purposively to its environment; and

Problems are resolved as they arise.[11]

The definitions of Likert and Miles suggest that there is more—or, to be precise, less—to participation than the satisfaction of personal needs of participants; they must be satisfied within the needs of the organization.

Halpin, however, taking a cue from Likert's early work at the Institute for Social Research at the University of Michigan,[12] defined climate in terms of management styles.[13] He identified six different climates:

1. Open-collegial.
2. Autonomous—laissez-faire.
3. Controlled—task-oriented.
4. Familiar—a happy family.
5. Paternal—father knows best.
6. Closed—mechanistic and controlled.

The pitfalls of the Halpin approach can be inferred by examining a statement of Tannenbaum and Massarik: "No leadership is inherently effective or ineffective; it might be either, depending on the goals with reference to which it is assessed."[14]

Carefully reviewing these various definitions of what constitutes an organizational climate conducive to fostering full employee participation, it would appear that what is being described is a constructive tension between the organization and the workforce—a dynamic process in which a clear, but subtle, balance must be maintained. It is this balance which the personnel department must honor if it is to pursue successfully its activities affecting employee participation in the organization.

The Personnel Department and Employee Participation

The Likert and Miles formulations seem to place the responsibility for employee participation on the administration. As a significant part of the administrative process, the personnel department must exhibit its sensitivity to the balance between organizational and employee needs in decisions concerning personnel recruitment, selection, assignment, evaluation, and development. Indeed, the skills with which the balance is maintained should be evident in all facets of employee relationships, whether collective bargaining, grievance hearings, wage and salary administration, employee benefits programs, or employee counseling. In view of this, it seems reasonable that the personnel department is the agency most often asked to conduct surveys to determine organizational climate. A typical set of survey questions addressing this concern is shown in figure 7-2.

If the survey technique is used, a number of constraints should be kept in mind. First, personnel responses are generally more likely to be accurate if they are anonymous. If there is reason to suspect the integrity of the personnel department (such as putting too much weight on one or the other of the scales maintaining the balance), an exterior consultant should be asked to conduct the survey. To be useful, responses should be keyed to the department or building to which the respondent is assigned. The survey responses are not meant to be a measure of the extent of personnel satisfaction; they are useful only in locating subjects and places in which organizational climate is being assessed. They may be useful to the organization to the extent they are followed up in the places indicated and about the subjects that are in doubt. The follow-up may prompt several kinds of inquiry.

Inquiry to determine the causes of an apparent breakdown in employee participation may take one or more of the following forms, regardless of the source of the information:

Interaction with other community educational agencies.

Performance appraisals of teachers, administrators, or other personnel.

Role definitions and task assignments.

Recruiting, selection, assignment, and evaluation procedures.

Collective bargaining practices.

Grievance hearing practices.

Employee compensation and benefits.

Inquiry information and follow-up data should be transmitted to the administrators of the units in which the organizational climate is in question. This evidence of commitment to maximum employee participation may lend credence to the organization's goals for human resource development. This may include the development of skills.

Organizational Commitment to Skill Development

In school administration, the importance of skill development to human resource development can hardly be overstated. The reasons prompting this statement may well be found within the profession itself. A conclusion reached by Sergiovanni after his replication with teachers of a Herzberg study on motivation addressed the situation as follows:

> Teaching offers little opportunity for concrete advancement [change in status or position] and in fact any particular teaching assignment could be considered as a terminal position. Whatever potential the factor, advancement, has as a satisfier appears to be lost for teachers under our present system. Capitalizing on this factor, as a potential source of satisfaction, implies providing overt opportunities for advancement within the ranks of teachers.[15]

It would appear that this is a first-order priority in human resource development in school administration.

Skills Mastery as Advancement

But a status structure of some sort must be built to reinforce the individual's need to progress. Such a structure should be related to the development of skills, that is, upon the individual's ability to perform as a professional in his field. Wherever identification of skills necessary to task completion—and their ranking in order of difficulty—has been done during the evaluation process, a basis exists for a status system. Rank ordering skills can be done in at least five orders of difficulty: (1) minimal (for task acceptance), (2) required (for continued employment), (3) desirable (for all experienced teachers), (4) outstanding (for coaching of other teachers), and (5) exceptional (gained by only a few and used to develop evaluation coaches). It is probably true that the value of the status system rests on the satisfaction the teacher receives in (finally) mastering the most difficult skills of the profession. Clearly, then, (1) the skill must be accurately labeled, and (2) its existence must be accurately established. If these conditions are not met, there is danger in the thwarting of the ultimate satisfaction of the teacher; and there is danger—perhaps more so—if the system mistakenly attaches the label to all tasks that a teacher accepts when it is ap-

ORGANIZATIONAL CLIMATE SURVEY

Please place an X in the box preceding the one statement in each group of four choices which best represents your opinion.

1. To what extent are you aware of the educational objectives of your school system?
   (1) I feel that, generally speaking, I am unaware of these objectives ☐
   (2) Sometimes I feel that I am aware of these objectives, but at other times I feel hopelessly "lost." ☐
   (3) I usually feel that I am aware of these objectives. ☐
   (4) I am confident that I am always aware of these objectives. ☐

2. To what extent do you accept these objectives as goals worth working toward?
   (1) I believe that these objectives are, for the most part, basically unsound. ☐
   (2) I believe these objectives to be of limited value only. ☐
   (3) I believe that most of the objectives are of value. ☐
   (4) I believe that all of the objectives are of value. ☐

3. To what extent do you believe that these objectives can be achieved?
   (1) I believe that, under present circumstances, none of the objectives can be achieved. ☐
   (2) I believe that only a few are likely to be achieved; and these after much effort. ☐
   (3) I believe that most of the objectives will be achieved. ☐
   (4) I believe that all of the objectives will be achieved. ☐

4. To what extent do you have confidence that you are doing, and will continue to do, all you can to achieve these objectives?
   (1) I feel that, most of the time, I am not putting forth my best efforts. ☐
   (2) I feel that I have been putting forth good effort in this direction, but feel that my efforts will diminish in the future. ☐
   (3) I feel that I have been, and shall continue, to put forth some effort. ☐
   (4) I feel that, beyond all doubt, I shall continue to put forth all my effort to achieve these objectives. ☐

5. To what extent do you feel that others with whom you work are doing, and will continue to do, all they can do to achieve these objectives?
   (1) They feel that, most of the time, they are not putting forth their best efforts. ☐
   (2) They feel that they have been putting forth good efforts in this direction, but feel that their efforts will diminish in the future. ☐
   (3) They feel that they have been putting forth and shall continue to put forth some effort. ☐
   (4) They feel that, beyond all doubt, they should continue to put forth all their efforts to achieve these objectives. ☐

6. To what extent do you have confidence in the capacity and sincerity of the present school administrators as leaders who can direct your efforts in the achievement of these objectives?
   (1) I feel that the present administrators are limited in both capacity and sincerity. ☐
   (2) I feel that they are reasonably capable but are somewhat lacking in sincerity. ☐
   (3) I feel that they are both reasonably capable and sincere. ☐
   (4) I have complete confidence in their capacity and sincerity. ☐

7. To what extent do you have confidence in the ability and sincerity of the citizens of the community to assist the professional staff in discovering and defining the reasonable objectives of the school system?
   (1) I feel that the citizens are limited both in ability and sincerity. ☐
   (2) I feel that they are reasonably able but are somewhat lacking in sincerity. ☐
   (3) I feel that they are reasonably able and reasonably sincere. ☐
   (4) I have complete confidence in their ability and sincerity. ☐

8. If educational trends in your school system continue for the next ten years as they have been going in the past ten years, what are the chances that the School System will be among the best public school systems in the country?
   (1) Very little chance ☐
   (2) Some chance but rather remote ☐
   (3) A fair chance ☐
   (4) A very good chance ☐

Developed by Claude W. Fawcett, Professor of Education, University of California, Los Angeles.

Figure 7-2. Organizational Climate Survey

propriate for only one or two. Obviously, some teachers can be exceptional in completing one task, but have minimal skills in others. And the system allows only an identification of the teacher's status in relation to a designated task. Still, the building of a status system—even an accurate, trusted one—may have a hollow meaning unless supported by a viable inservice development program

Inservice Development

It is unlikely that a viable inservice program can be developed unless all costs incurred by the employee are borne by the employer. The often-heard charge that this is a "gift of public monies" stems from the scientific administration policy of placing development responsibility on the employee. But even if the costs were to be borne by the employer, the program should be directed by policies different from those presently being used. Some new policies, reflecting skill development possibilities in inservice programs, are suggested here:

> The burden of inservice development is properly carried by the collegial coaching procedure recommended in the chapter on performance appraisal. Included may be demonstrations, observations, workshops with persons trying to master the same skills, or experimentation alone or with others.
>
> If departments of education participate in inservice development, their participation should consist of two- to five-day instruction periods devoted to the demonstration of a new method, the use of new tools or materials, or a discussion and analysis of a new discovery.
>
> If Teacher Centers[16] are used, their inservice contribution should be limited to curriculum development and experimentation with students not available in the employing district.
>
> If achieving familiarity with a community subculture is a part of skill development, leaders of the subculture should be invited to assist the teacher, or group of teachers, and help them to participate in community activities to share the community cultural heritage.

These policies will serve to reinforce the meaning of the status system and provide inservice opportunities directly related to skill development.

Not all teachers, however, are dedicated to the development of outstanding or exceptional teaching skills. Some may find greater satisfaction in seeking administrative or specialist positions as a means of advancement, although the number of such positions is small and the risks to the present teacher are great.

Management and Specialist Development

The risks involved to the teacher interested in an administrative or specialist position are relative to the need to develop skills other than those required for better teaching. In all districts, moreover, there is intense competition for the new administrative and specialist positions available. Further, there is no guarantee that, once up the ladder, steady progression will follow. For example, an ambitious specialist or administrator may compete successfully for less demanding positions, but eventually fail to secure appointment to more responsible assignments. When the upward mobility stops, he faces a set of Hobson's choices. He can swallow his pride and remain on a shelf (that is, hold the same or similar position) for the rest of his career. He can return to teaching at the cost of resuming his professional career among colleagues who have not taken the detour of attempting to qualify for another profession. He can seek administrative or specialist placement in another educational organization. Or he can abandon the educational professions and seek employment elsewhere. These are serious risks, and a reasoned evaluation of their importance may make him reluctant to join a development program, particularly if status advancement within teaching is available. Yet educational employers do need a reliable source of supply for administrative and specialist personnel. And the most reliable source, as discussed in an earlier chapter, is the workforce of the organization. It appears, then, that a well thought out development program may serve to minimize the risks to both the employees and the district. But generating such a program requires carefully constructed policies for selection and placement.

Selection

Selection of participants in administrative or specialist development programs is essential to minimizing their risks. Participation of individuals with marginal qualifications may eventually cost the employee a chance for promotion in teaching, or the district a valued employee. And the customary recommendation that evidence of administrative potential be provided in each evaluation report appears to be a simplistic solution. Only those who have potential, and are willing to take the risk, should be included. The estimation of risk by the employee requires that he be provided the following information to guide his and the district's decision:

> The beginning administrative and specialist positions, the number of incumbents, the expected number of vacancies in the subsequent five years and the minimal skills for entry into each.
>
> Each position in the normal promotion sequence from the beginning position to the top assignment, the number of current incumbents in each, the expected number of vacancies in each in the subsequent five years, and minimal skills for entry into each.
>
> Program procedures for the development of skills, for example, position rotation, internships, externships in other organizations, or experimentation.
>
> District support for program participation, for example, released time at district expense, tuition costs, books and materials costs, internship and externship costs, cooperation in research, and adjustments in

teaching salaries in the event of nonappointment or withdrawal from the program.

The last item of support is crucial. The participant may view it as compensation for the risk he is taking. From the employer's point of view, the willingness to support the participant creates an organizational obligation not only to restrict participation to the able and willing, but to terminate participation promptly when there is a failure to progress. But even the most carefully conceived and effectively operated program—because of scarcity of personnel losses and uncertainty about vacancies—will always provide more personnel than the organization can use. And the attractiveness of the program may depend on how well-prepared, but unused, graduates are placed by the organization.

Placement

A number of placement options may be used to enhance the willingness of employees to participate in the administrative and specialist development program—even if some of the participants cannot be used in the positions available in the district. They can be described as follows:

> Because only large organizations are likely to have the resources to mount a development program, the organization—through its personnel department—can actively seek to place unused graduates in other educational organizations.
>
> Occupants of shelf positions who prefer to remain in the organization may be asked to provide instructional services in the programs they have completed, to act as consultants in the resolution of organizational problems, or serve as interim occupants of administrative positions.
>
> If graduates prefer to return to teaching, they should be able to do so without a reduction in salary even if the salary is one of a shelf position.

These policies may be viewed as further, partial compensation for risks taken in entering the program, thus encouraging participation.

Organizational Reinforcement of Desirable Employee Behavior

In his replication with teachers of Herzberg's study of motivation, Sergiovanni suggested that three areas in which teachers found their dominant satisfactions were (1) achievement, (2) recognition, and (3) responsibility.[17] For reinforcement in all three areas, organizations have characteristically relied on feedback from principals, supervisors, students, parents, and colleagues. Of itself, this extrinsic reward system which took the form of letters, oral statements, gifts, and committee assignments, proved insufficient. There was no other, however. What is suggested here is the need to develop an intrinsic system, a series of steps offering the teacher the possibility of finding satisfaction from his own values. But such a program cannot be developed without modifyng or interrupting the continuity of many traditional practices.

Achievement

Every teacher can cite instances in which he left a classroom in such a state of euphoria that he could declare, "I know I knocked them dead today!" And each can cite days in which he left despondent with the feeling, "I blew it completely today." Most teachers indulge, at some time or other, in the feeling of having contributed something—usually more than is justified—to the professional success of a former student. Lortie described these reactions as "psychic gratifications."[18] But, whatever the name, they are mere straws in the wind of professional uncertainty.

Human resource development requires a more substantial procedure for assessing achievement and providing intrinsic reinforcement. It is suggested that if learning goals for each student are clearly specified, the teaching process that accomplished these goals may then provide a basis for self-evaluation of achievement. What this step requires is individualization of instruction—a cooperative process of student-teacher joint effort in the successive development of mutually recognized goals. By rank ordering the student goals, a sequence of cooperation can be established. When student evaluations are conducted, they should look for the presence of a skill sought, a behavior intended to be developed, or the use of knowledge expected. Thus, it becomes possible for both the teacher and the student to measure achievement and receive reinforcement. But this student-teacher evaluation system does not provide for the recognition sought by the teacher.

Recognition

Special notice or attention that motivates intrinsically is most likely to be provided by members of the profession. An expression of approval, recognition signifies that the teacher is acting as an effective and well-trained professional. The organization can facilitate this by its choice of evaluation procedures. If evaluation is, indeed, viewed as a process of collegial coaching devoted to the substantiation of acquired skills, a communication link with the profession is provided. Professional support can be expanded into organizational recognition if evaluation reports are used by it to detemine assignments—give responsibility to those who have demonstrated competence.

Responsibility

A teacher's sense of responsibility (read, independent professional choice of action) has all too often been blunted by any one of several things—organizational prescription of rules, regulations, curricula, methods, and interactions with parents. But every teacher knows that learning is done by students, not supervisors, administrators, or parents, and that all students do not require the same instructional treatment. State regulations concerning minimum competencies, standardized testing, and procedural relations may contribute to the teacher's feeling of frustrated compliance. An emphasis on professional determination of appropriate instructional practice—in conjunction with individual instruction and collegial evaluation—may tend to restore some satisfaction to the teacher in the acceptance of responsibility.

Summary

Organizations that consider employees to be capital assets often create human resource development programs to add value. In doing so, an attempt is made not only to free individuals to work enthusiastically on tasks that they value and contribute maximally to the goal accomplishment of the organization, but to achieve their own personal goals and derive maximum personal satisfaction from the activity. In accomplishing these ends, the educational organization is required to define its role in the community educational program, define the subgoals of each unit, and define the subgoals of the unit to be assigned to each employee. And the subgoals assigned should be recognized by the employee as a coherent part not only of the unit and district's tasks, but of the community's educational program. In accepting these tasks, the employee is entitled to opportunities for full participation in all aspects of the cooperative community and district endeavor.

The ability of the employee to participate fully depends upon the maintenance of an organizational climate conducive to participation. A favorable climate is characterized by a dynamic educational values consensus, functional role definitions, collegial interaction, an effective communication system, maximum resource utilization, positive organizational response to its environment, and creativity. If such a climate exists, the organization requires a positive program for skill development.

Skill development by teachers may be facilitated by the adoption of a status system created to provide recognition of advancement in the profession. The development of administrative or specialist skills may require the establishment of a development program carefully organized to minimize the risks to the district and the employees. If risks can be minimized, the availability of professional administrative and specialist skills can be enhanced. But even these major steps in human resource development may leave employees dissatisfied.

There are no comparable lighthouse programs for assuring teacher satisfaction in achievement, recognition, and responsibility. The individualization of instruction and collegial evaluation may tend to restore a sense of professional responsibility for the educational development of students.

Notes

1. E.W. Bakke, *The Fusion Process* (New Haven, Conn.: The Yale University Labor and Management Center, 1955).
2. Management Responsibility Guidance Corporation, *Project Interaction: A Manual for Use of the Management Responsibility Guide* (Los Angeles: The Corporation, 1974).
3. Reprinted, by permission of the publisher, from "Roles and Relationships: Clarifying the Manager's Job," Robert D. Melcher, *Personnel* 44 (1967):33-41. © 1967 by American Management Association, Inc. All rights reserved.
4. P.R. Lawrence and J.W. Lorsch, *Organization and Environment: Managing Differentiation and Integration* (Cambridge, Mass.: Harvard Graduate School of Business Administration, 1967).
5. Cyril Sofer, "Reactions to Administrative Change: A Study of Staff Relations in Three British Hospitals," *Human Relations* 8 (1955):291-316.
6. John Logue, "On the Road toward Worker-Run Companies?: The Employee Participation Act in Practice," in *Working Life in Sweden* (New York: Swedish Information Service, 1978).
7. George S. McIsaac, "What's Coming in Labor Relations?" *Harvard Business Review* 55 (1977):22.
8. *Statistical Abstract of the United States,* 97th ed. (Washington, D.C.: U.S. Bureau of the Census, 1976), pp. 356, 384.

9. William L. Batt, Jr., and Edgar Weinberg, "Labor-Management Cooperation Today," *Harvard Business Review* 56 (1978):96.

10. Rensis Likert, "The Nature of Highly Effective Groups," in *Organizations and Human Behavior,* eds. Fred D. Carver and Thomas J. Sergiovanni (New York: McGraw-Hill, 1969), pp. 356-367.

11. Matthew B. Miles, "Planned Change and Organizational Health: Figure and Ground," in *Organizations and Human Behavior,* eds. Fred D. Carver and Thomas J. Sergiovanni (New York: McGraw-Hill, 1969), pp. 375-391.

12. Robert C. Allbrook, "Participative Management: Time for a Second Look," *Fortune* 75 (1967):167.

13. Andrew W. Halpin, *Theory and Research in Administration* (New York: Macmillan, 1966), pp. 174-181.

14. Robert Tannenbaum and Fred Massarik, "Leadership: A Frame of Reference," *Management Science* 4 (1957):126-129.

15. Thomas J. Sergiovanni, "Factors Which Affect Satisfaction and Dissatisfaction of Teachers," in *Organizations and Human Behavior,* eds. Fred D. Carver and Thomas J. Sergiovanni (New York: McGraw-Hill, 1969), pp. 249-260.

16. Robert M. Caldwell, "Transplanting the British Teacher Center in the U.S.," *Phi Delta Kappan* 60 (1979):517-520.

17. Sergiovanni, "Satisfaction and Dissatisfaction of Teachers," p. 256.

18. Dan Lortie, "The Changing Role of Teachers as a Result of Such Innovations as Television, Programmed Instruction, and Team Teaching," in *The Administrative Analysis of Selected Educational Innovations,* eds. Richard Lonsdale and Carl Steinhoff. Report of the First Interuniversity Conference for School Administrators, Syracuse University, 1964.

8 Collective Bargaining

Since conflict is inherent in human association, it follows that conflicts in educational organizations are similar to those in any other group-related endeavor. Most conflicts arise, apparently, from differences stemming from an "optic," a point of view. Many occurring in education may be described in rather concise terms, as follows:

Joint effort: malfunctioning in cooperation.

Alienation: differences concerning organizational decisions.

Status: role conflicts.

Recognition: differences concerning the value of personal efforts and accomplishments.

Advancement: differences concerning promotions.

Equity: differences over equal organizational treatment.

Institutional evaluation: differences concerning group progress and accomplishments.

Creativity: differences concerning freedom to use initiative.

Causes: differences of personal convictions.

Personality: disappointments with the behavior of colleagues.

Since conflict, like all manifestations of human behavior, is caused by differences among people, the manner in which it is resolved becomes the pivotal issue in any system of administration designed to secure results based on cooperation among many contributing elements. It is, then, joint effort that is central to administrative action. It may well be that conflict is produced by the persistent efforts of individuals to maintain a sense of personal worth despite the loss of autonomy required in joint effort.

Each time in the twentieth century that political, social, and economic pressures have slowly, but inexorably, forced changes in administrative styles, a rationale and procedure for coping with organizational conflict—a way of maintaining organizational health—has been developed. Earliest was scientific administration; the employee was considered an entrepreneur.

In direct consequence of this point of view, any conflict between the employee and the organization was logically resolved by his personal negotiation with the administrators of the organization. The various areas of difference were handled within this context. Going down the list—a list by no means exhaustive—alienation was perceived as unresolvable and caused voluntary or organizational termination. But discussions with the "boss" were necessary for almost everything else: participation in decision-making, maintenance of status, trying out new methods, securing advancement, finding out what the organization was doing. Further, administrative disciplinary action, following negotiations with administrators, was customary for enforcing cooperation; equity was maintained by negotiations about work standards; and recognition, all too often, required persistent effort to point out to administrators the results of exceptional effort.

Examining the scientific administration type of conflict resolution closely, it became apparent that the balance between employer and employees was weighted heavily on the side of the administrators and the organization. Even if organizational physical size—as separate from a multi-administrative unit—had not precluded the feasibility of individual negotiations, administrative perception of the employee as an entrepreneur (or a single unit force, looking out for his own economic well-being) would have required him to become an almost indispensable individual to have reasonable power in negotiations with an administrator. It would seem logical, under such conditions, that the human relations approach to administration was developed as an attempt to achieve a sense of balance between the employee and administrators. And the human relations theorists endorsed group action to restore balance; this led a rapid growth of unionism. Collective bargaining became the technique for a balanced resolution of conflict.

The justification for federal laws establishing the federally sponsored collective bargaining process emphasized this reason for its endorsement. In supporting the first federal collective bargaining act—the Wagner Act of 1935—Chief Justice Hughes wrote the majority decision of the U.S. Supreme Court in *National Labor Relations Board* v. *Jones and Laughlin Steel Corporation* in 1937. He stated that

> [unions] were organized out of the necessities of the situation; that a single employee was helpless in dealing with an employer; that he was dependent ordinarily on his daily wage for the maintenance of himself and his family; that if the employer refused to pay him the wages he thought fair, he was nevertheless unable to leave the employ and resist arbitrary and unfair treatment; that union was essential to give laborers opportunity to deal on an equality with employers.[1]

Much the same argument was used by Senator Robert Taft in 1947 in arguing for the passage of the Labor Management Relations Act (Taft-

Hartley Bill), which is today's basic collective bargaining law. Taft stated the purpose as follows:

> Before the passage of any of these laws, the employer undoubtedly had an advantage in dealing with his employees. He was one man; the employees might be thousands; and he could deal with them one at a time. In negotiations of that character he had such a superior advantage that Congress came to feel that it must legislate specifically in order to correct that situation and bring about a balance. Congress passed the Clayton Act and the Norris-LaGuardia Act in order to limit legal actions against unions. Congress passed the Wagner National Labor Relations Act in order that the employees of a single employer might act as one in dealing with one employer, in order that they might be on a sound and equal basis, a principle which I think no one can question and which certainly is not questioned in the pending bill.[2]

In creating a collective bargaining system, therefore, it was the intent of Congress to create a conflict resolution system under law which would assure the public of an orderly method of group negotiations with employers. It is, perhaps, worthy of note that both the Wagner Act and the Taft-Hartley Act were passed during the period of greatest enthusiasm for the human relations system of administrative thought (circa 1930-1957).

As representatives of all members of the union, negotiators found that demands had to be restricted to those issues considered important by the majority; conflicts with less than majority support were strategically omitted from the bargaining process. Walter Reuther recognized this problem and stated the union's position succinctly as follows: "You cannot strike General Motors on individual grievances. I don't want to tie up 90,000 workers because one worker was laid off for two months."[3]

Thus, in an effort to reconcile individual needs and group requirements within the union framework, labor expanded its scope of bargaining both in the private and public sector. But although the unions often included in negotiations most broad disputes with management, there were still a number of conflicts that could not be considered—and these were frequently crucial to goal accomplishment. Once again, an adjustment was needed to respond to evolving needs and requirements. A broader view of conflict resolution, one that included consideration of nonbargaining conflicts, was provided by the social systems school of administrative thought.

The social systems concept of organizational conflict was described as follows by Sofer in discussing industrial organizations:

> Organizational conflict in the industrial firm is normal and usual, an integral aspect of the enterprise that cannot be removed or eradicated from the system. The industrial organization is an area of conflict as well as collaboration, a coalition of individuals and subgroups simultaneously united by the prospect of common benefits derivable from the enterprise and divided by conflicts of interests, definition, and perception.[4]

And it was the acceptance of this definition of organizational conflict that led to the recommendation of acceptance of Brooks Adam's definition of administrative thought (described in chapter 1). It is a rationale of administrative thinking that deserves repetition here. According to Adams, administration is "the ability to coordinate many, often conflicting, social energies so adroitly that they operate as a unity."[5] It is also the rationale for recommending personnel actions in educational organizations used throughout this text. Examining the delineation of points of differences listed earlier in this chapter, a brief summary of the social system's contribution to the resolution of conflict will demonstrate the necessity of integrating personnel administration and collective bargaining as two facets of a single conflict resolution system. Thus, in the context of the social systems approach to administration, a description of conflict resolution recommendations would include

Joint effort: assignments that provide a definition of cooperative effort in the organization.

Alienation: the building of a dynamic educational beliefs consensus and its use in determining objectives will enable the organization to assign valued tasks to employees.

Status: assignment procedures must provide the means of resolving role conflicts.

Recognition: the evaluations system should be based on reinforcement of desired behavior, redirection of inadequate behavior, and development of the capability of self-evaluation.

Advancement: skill development in the human resource programs will provide the rationale for advancement not only in teaching, but in promotion to non-teaching assignments.

Equity: an emphasis on task assignment within the skills of the employee, advancement as more difficult skills are acquired, participation in the development of goals, recognition for skills attained, independence in completing assigned tasks, support from interested colleagues, and support from administrators are essential to provide a framework for the perception of equity.

Institutional evaluation: the planning process must require the sharp definition of the criteria (goals) for evaluating progress.

Creativity: the evaluation procedures must provide an opportunity for encouraging creative behavior in task completion.

Causes: the dynamic process of maintaining an educational beliefs consensus should provide opportunities for individuals to present the meanings of their convictions for educational action.

Personality: orientation that provides the employee an insight concerning the expected behavior of colleagues, thereby tending to diminish surprises in their association, and reducing negative reactions.

These recommendations demonstrate that the personnel department—in the completion of its assigned tasks—is already deeply involved in conflict resolution. The department, therefore, has a substantial interest in collective bargaining in which agreements may contribute to—or detract from—the ability to carry on its regular work. As a result, it is fair to conclude that the personnel department should assume a positive role in the process that is not now commonly assumed. This requires, among other actions, a clearer determination of the personnel department's relations with the negotiator.

Relations with the Negotiator

Collective bargaining is, characteristically, a transaction between two negotiators. In school negotiations these are (1) the school negotiator who, according to a 1979 Rand study, is most often a professional employed for the purpose, generally, either an attorney specializing in labor relations or a specialist in industrial relations; and (2) the union negotiator, usually a full-time union employee. The district negotiator is supported by a team headed by the personnel director; others on the district team are usually a district finance officer and school principals. The union negotiator is supported by the head of the union and representative teachers.[6] The teams constituted in this manner have (1) tended to equalize the expertise of the two chief negotiators; (2) provided each with support individuals who could secure quickly the needed data; and (3) enabled the two negotiators, when they worked easily together, to make rapid "trade offs" essential to and characteristic of the bargaining process. As for the board of education involvement, it is often restricted to "reservation points" and "concessions," thus leaving the teams to resolve the conflict.

But the procedure, however efficient, limited the participation of teachers and the public; in effect, their contributions were confined to the preparation of original demands. There have been many attempts to involve both of these groups more fully in the bargaining itself. These attempts, referred to as "sunshine laws," have not thus far been notably successful.

Sunshine Laws

The landmark law aimed at including employees and the public in bargaining was passed in Florida in 1974. Termed "fishbowl" bargaining, it opened to the public view all bargaining sessions, with the exception of those which had reached impasse and had required mediation. Various states enacted versions of this type of law: Wisconsin, as of January 1, 1978, required open meetings in two situations: (1) for the presentation of original proposals, and (2) after mediation had failed to resolve an impasse.[7] California, with the Rodda Act of 1974, required both employees and employers to present their initial proposals at a public meeting.[8] New Jersey and Iowa courts ruled that open bargaining was permissible if both parties agreed to it. Little consistency, however, can be found among the various laws. A 1975 study conducted in Florida showed that no significant public participation had been secured there, even though the news media had attended seven out of ten of all bargaining sessions conducted in Florida during the first year of the "sunshine" law.[9] It is fair to conclude that, to date, attempts at broadening particiption beyond the professional negotiating teams are either in a preliminary state of development or inconsistent with the process itself.

If this conclusion is justified, it follows that

> The designation of the personnel administrator, or a member of his staff, as the negotiator will not change substantially the extent of public or employee participation.
>
> The restriction of participation will limit the scope of bargaining to matters of general concern to both the public and the employees.
>
> The incorporation of bargaining into the whole system of conflict resolution depends on the kinds and quality of personnel department participation.

And one essential kind of departmental participation is the appointment of the personnel director as the chairman of the negotiating team. But to be most effective in that role, the personnel director must have conducted many of the preparatory steps to bargaining.

Preparation for Bargaining

Preparation for bargaining may have begun as early as the formation of units, as well as collecting data necessary for the bargaining process.

Unit Formation

A bargaining unit is unlikely to command full participation by its members unless they choose it with full understanding of (1) the role of collective bargaining in the conflict resolution process of the school district, (2) its potential, (3) its limitations, and (4) its costs both to the union and the district. Understanding of these facts and the presentation of them to employees contemplating entering collective bargaining will produce the desirable result, at least, of having union organizers answer them. The ensuing debate may not prevent the formation of a bargaining unit, but the discussion may develop a more sophisticated and complete participation in union affairs by its members. In performing this service, the personnel department is required to refrain from any act that would interfere with the employee's free choice. The general policy on district informational activity of this type is spelled out in the U.S. Labor Management Relations Act of 1947 (Taft-Hartley Bill) and repeated in the same or similar language in most state laws. It allows "the expressing of any views, arguments, or opinions or the dissemination thereof, whether in printed, graphic, or visual form."[10] Fulmer reported that the usual organizational procedures in providing employees information about unions when they are deciding about collective bargaining included meetings, letters to employees, employee surveys, posters, telephone calls, and supervisory counseling.[11] If, after considering the matter, the employees wanted to have a bargaining unit, the personnel department may have had to use persuasion to influence the formation of appropriate units.

An appropriate unit should include employees whose interests are substantially the same. If a unit has a more diverse group of people, some people will not be represented. It is clearly inappropriate, for example, to include in a unit both supervisors and the people they supervise. Secretaries or others privy to the affairs of the negotiating committee are equally inappropriate members of a union of other classifed employees. Further, the personnel department often feels required to keep the number of bargaining units to a minimum to conserve negotiating time. A school district, for example, often employs members of a number of craft unions (for example, plumbers, carpenters, bus drivers, painters, plasterers, and laborers). It is appropriate to urge these members of diverse craft unions to abandon their former memberships and form one union of classified employees.

If persuasion does not succeed in securing voluntary formation of appropriate units, an appeal to the state Public Employee Relations Board (Commission) is often permitted, as in the California Rodda Act of 1975, which specified:

> In each case where the appropriateness of the unit is an issue the [PERB] board shall decide the question on the basis of the community of interest between and among the employees and their established practices, including, among other things, the extent to which such employees belong to the same employee organization, and the effect of the size of the unit on the efficient operation of the school district.[12]

But another issue of whether a unit should be formed may arise. For example, principals of schools who pose the question of forming a separate bargaining unit. An extreme instance of this was the case of the San Francisco Unified School District principals who formed an organization affiliated with the Teamsters Union, although most other principal units that were formed had affiliated with the AFL-CIO. By early 1975, 1,015 school administrator locals had been formed, almost all in eight states (Connecticut, New Jersey, Washington, New York, Massachusetts, Michigan, Pennsylvania, and Ohio). Only in Connecticut and New Jersey were the unions strong enough to enroll a majority of school administrators.[13] When such a union is permitted by law, it becomes the responsibility of the personnel department to point persuasively to the possible impairment of other conflict resolution activities assumed by principals. But regardless of the department's questioning of unit formation, it must assume organizational obligations in the process of their formation.

Procedural tasks of the personnel department in the establishment of bargaining units may be described as follows:

Maintenance of employee access to union information either through facilitation of mail distribution or scheduling of meetings.

Participation in union certification by provision of lists of proposed unit members, dues check-off confirmations, or facilitation of the circulation of petitions.

Facilitation of the PERB elections among employees when required.

Collecting Data for Bargaining

If collective bargaining is to accomplish its intended conflict resolution purposes, both unions and employers should enter the process fully prepared. It is the personnel department's assigned task to collect the appropriate data to make this possible. Miller has supplied the categories of needed data; their interpretation by the author for schools is indicated in an accompanying column, as shown in table 8-1.

Miller also pointed out that this type of thorough preparation is not universally done. In his study of ten large manufacturing firms, three nonprofit medical centers, and two municipal governments, he found that nine reacted only to union proposals; they did not see the development of management plans desirable.[14] A reasonable concern for securing a positive gain from negotiations would seem to suggest not only that preparation be done, but that some of the information developed should be shared with the union.

Sharing information with the union may indeed have desirable effects,

Table 8-1
Data Needed for Collective Bargaining

Category	*School District Interpretation*
Audit of grievances	A tabulation of grievances filed, arbitrators' decisions, and possible contract amendments that might be made to diminish the incidence of grievances.
Contract analysis	Comparisons with contracts of other educational employers competing for the same personnel, and determination of amendments more nearly conforming to district desires.
Anticipation of adversarial demands	An analysis of statements of union leaders, demands made of other employers, actions taken by boards of education, and union positions taken in grievance hearings.
Updating of personnel and compensation data	Information regarding characteristics of the workforce, wage payments and premiums, benefit payments, benefit costs, statutory costs, and worker performance.
Appointment of a coordinating committee	Members should usually include the personnel director, a finance officer, and representative principals and supervisors.
Coordination with other employers	Conduct an analysis of the negotiation plans of other employers, often facilitated by an association of employers.
Contingency planning	Preparation should be made in advance for alternative responses to different union demands expected in negotiations.
Consultation with administrators	Full participation should be secured from top and middle management personnel not only in the preparation of the negotiation plan, but also during negotiations that may alter aspects of the original plan.
Review of worker utilization	Personnel moves should be anticipated, including the possibilities that certain activities may be phased out, staff may be reduced, or different assignments may be contemplated.
Refinement of bargaining strategy	Anticipation of strategy changes in response to different union strategies.
Briefing of the board of directors	All data prepared for negotiations should be shared with the board of education, since only the board can approve a contract.

Source: Categories taken from Ronald L. Miller, "Preparations for Negotiations," *Personnel Journal* 57 (1978):36-39.

but it should not interfere with the anticipated benefits of the adversarial examination of alternatives. Some adversarial benefits might be lost if planning data were exchanged (1) concerning the anticipated union demands, (2) negotiation plans of other employers, (3) possible responses to union demands, (4) bargaining strategies, or (5) positions of members of the board of education. But there are others that do provide a common data base for constructive disagreement. These are (1) the grievance audit, (2) contract analyses, (3) worker utilization information, (4) the membership of the district's negotiation committee, (5) personnel characteristics and compensation data, and (6) time sequences for bargaining. Still, care should be taken that cooperation with the union in creating a framework for collective bargaining should not mean a softening of the personnel department's adversarial role in the conduct of negotiations.

Participation in Negotiations

The maintenance of a strong adversarial position by the school district is necessary if positive benefits are to be gained from collective bargaining. The process is effective only if both parties have equal power, pursue their choices of alternatives with equal vigor, and are willing to exchange a concession for an equal concession by the opposing party. Much of the power of the employer rests in the legal obligation of the board of education to conduct schools regardless of the conflicts that develop. This obligation, inherent in state delegation of powers to local school districts, is further reinforced by the provisions of educational collective bargaining laws in thirty-three states. Only six of the thirty-three state laws authorize strikes by educational employees and each of the six specify somewhat stringent restrictions for the exercise of the right.[15] The obligation of the board of trustees to continue instruction as long as there is a viable corps of nonstriking employees available is tenable because (1) not all conflicts with unions are legitimate, (2) some cannot be resolved at a particular period of time, and (3) some can never be completely resolved. In the maintenance of instruction, the personnel department must provide a staff of qualified substitutes.

Substitutes

Since withdrawal of services by educational employees during strikes is common—even if not legally authorized—a substitute list large enough to fill all positions that can be vacated must be maintained. Good faith in recruiting substitutes requires determining in advance their willingness to serve under strike conditions, and making provisions to protect their persons and property. Protection of substitutes may require the following:

> Strategic assignment of guards to parking lots, entrances, and isolated units on the school grounds.

Deployment of observers with cameras to strategic observation points on school property, and prompt referral of law violators to the police.

Recordings of sounds of disturbances on school grounds.

Maintenance of substitutes' telephone numbers as "confidential."

But even protective devices may not suffice to secure enough substitutes, and wholesale transfers of nonstriking personnel may be necessary.

Transfers may be used to staff a limited number of schools if the individuals available are too few to staff all. This may require prompt action by the personnel department at the outset of a strike. A likely transfer problem, however, is the reconstruction of a staff with substitutes. This may involve the movement of strategic nonstriking personnel who can provide leadership for substitutes, and this may well present a problem throughout the strike period. The redeployment of the staff adds urgency to the good faith obligation of the personnel department to keep both substitutes and nonstriking personnel informed of the progress of negotiations.

Strike Communications

One time-honored custom of collective bargaining has been the maintenance of the confidentiality of bargaining. This has, of course, been breached by the "sunshine" laws, but their infrequent application has often pushed the real negotiations into cloakrooms or closets to maintain confidentiality. But it is a tradition that has not restricted the communication to interested parties of issues under consideration, agreements reached, and issues yet unresolved—the kind of information that should be provided regularly to continuing employees.

Measures to maintain instruction serve to strengthen the adversarial position of the district negotiator, and the position is further reinforced by the personnel department's ability promptly to provide data concerning the effects of union proposals on personnel availability, development, and retention.

Participation in Negotiations

The contributions of the personnel department in assessing the organizational effects of different union proposals can be readily identified by examining the bargaining domains of the 100 sample districts reported in the 1979 Rand study. They were:

Grievance procedures;

School calendar and class hours;

Class size;

Teacher aides;

Teacher assignment;

Transfers;

Reductions in force;

Promotions;

Inservice and professional development;

Instructional policy;

Student grading and promotion;

Student discipline and teacher safety; and

Federal programs.[16]

The only domains outside the purview of the personnel department are (1) federal programs, (2) student grading and promotion, and (3) instructional policy. Projections of organizational consequences of modifications of district policies in all other domains are within the records potential of the department. And these projections can serve a useful purpose in assisting the personnel department to complete its tasks in contract administration.

Contract Administration

Collective bargaining agreements are incorporated into contracts that are legally enforced. Most laws authorizing collective bargaining for educational employees emphasize the binding nature of contracts in language similar to that of the California Rodda Act of 1975, as follows:

> Nothing in this section shall cause any court or the [PERB] board to hold invalid any negotiated agreement between public school employers and the exclusive representative entered into in accordance with the provisions of this Chapter.[17]

But some agreements were reached within an adversarial atmosphere. These then tended to possess (1) functional ambiguity in contract language to facilitate agreement, (2) unique interpretations restricted to the two bargaining teams present, and (3) self-serving interpretations by others not privy to the bargaining discussions. In this sense, therefore, a contract containing new or changed provisions may become a source of a growing stream of new conflicts unless the personnel department, working with district negotiators, attorneys, and negotiating committee members, in cooperation with their opposite numbers in the union, mount an information campaign, or are aware of other means, that will assure understanding of contract provisions by all.

Contract Interpretation

A first requirement in mounting an information campaign to minimize or avoid misunderstandings may well be the preparation of a contract administration manual. Such a written document or paper is particularly useful when both contracting parties agree on the meanings of the provisions for the behavior of administrators, boards of education, shop stewards (building and departmental representatives), and union officials. Since, oftentimes, this type of joint consultation has been known to degenerate into another, longer, and more complicated bargaining procedure, attention is usefully directed to broad statements of general responsibility rather than to specific acts illustrated with examples. The manual, when properly prepared, can be used as a teaching document in the district communication process.

A usual pattern of district communication includes (1) distribution of the manual to administrators and union representatives inviting questions concerning meanings not evident in the document; (2) group meetings in departments, decentralized units, and central offices; and (3) advertised meetings to which personnel interested in specific subjects are invited (for example, provisions for early retirement). These meetings tend to gain greater credibility for interpretations if they are conducted jointly by union and district representatives. But even the communication process, using the general recommendations of the manual, cannot anticipate accurately all of the different shadings of contract meaning that are likely to develop within the life of the contract. It becomes necessary, therefore, to develop a grievance procedure designed to adjudicate the differences that do arise.

Grievance Procedures

The obvious desirability of resolving differences as quickly as possible, even at the point of conflict, has caused Veglahn to identify two parts of the grievance process as "clinical" and "legalistic."[18] The clinical phase, according to Veglahn, is characterized by time limits and successive submission of the complaints, if unresolved, to various administrators in the hierarchy. A dramatic example of the importance of the time sequencing of labor disputes is the clinical procedure of the Detroit Public Schools as given in its 1967-1969 contract with Local 231 of the American Federation of Teachers, AFL-CIO.

In the Detroit contract, emphasis was placed, as it is in most such documents, on informal resolution with an immediate supervisor. If it were not resolved by informal means, a formal complaint was to be filed with the principal, who was obligated to discuss it with the grievant and a union representative. He was required to render a written decision within ten days, providing copies to the teacher and the union representative. If not satisfied, the grievant had ten days to appeal the principal's decision to the region superintendent. He was required to investigate the grievance by giving all parties to Step I an opportunity to be heard within ten days. Within fifteen days following the hearing, the region superintendent was required to render a written decision, providing supporting arguments, to the parties concerned. If the grievant was still not satisfied, he had ten days to appeal the decision to the superintendent of schools. Within ten days, the superintendent, or his designee, was required to give all parties to Step II an opportunity to be heard. Within fifteen days following the hearing, the superintendent was required to render a written decision to all concerned parties giving the reasons for his decision. If the grievant was still not satisfied, he had ten days in which to appeal the superintendent's decision to the board of education. The board had twenty days to give the union a hearing and render its decision. If the union was dissatisfied with the board's decision, it had twenty days to request advisory arbitration.[19]

In other school districts, not all steps as used in the Detroit system are mandated, nor do all districts have regional superintendents. Some require arbitration before referral to boards of education; some contracts include binding instead of advisory arbitration. But all clinical processes make failure to observe time sequences a tacit acceptance, by either party, of the decision in the final review. And all, in one way or another, provide for a "legalistic" system of adjudication of the dispute if the "clinical" process fails.

The "legalistic" system has, at times, been restricted to formal hearings conducted by the board of education. A board is a legislative body of a branch of state government and is vested with sovereign powers. Frequently, neither the board nor the people of the district wish to diminish its powers by contracting with the union to be bound by an arbitrator's decision.[20] But the final disposition of all grievances by a board of education is, at times, a long process. Its cumbersomeness serves to lessen the willingness of participants in the clinical process to resolve the conflict. And the perpetual difficulty of finding time for hearings in the calendar of the board causes delays in a process that requires prompt and equitable resolution. In an attempt at speeding up the process—while retaining the right of decision—boards have often agreed to "advisory" arbitration.

Advisory Arbitration

This is a contractual agreement that allows for the serious consideration of recommendations of a neutral hearing officer concerning the manner in which a grievance should be settled. In it, neither party gives up its right to pursue other remedies (that is, the board's right of decision or the union's right to include the issue in the agenda of the next bargaining session). The process of choosing a hearing officer, conduct of the hearing, and rendering the decision, however, is the same in advisory as binding arbitration.

Binding Arbitration

This is a contracted agreement in which both the union and the school district agree to accept the ruling of an unbiased hearing officer concerning the resolution of a grievance. A strict and formal arbitration process is characterized by the following:

Selection of an arbitrator from the membership of the American Arbitration Association by alternate striking of less favored arbitrators by the two parties until an arbitrator is chosen.

A prehearing to identify the issues under dispute.

The use of formal court hearing procedures (testimony taken under oath, rulings on evidence, direct questioning, cross examination, and summation).

Representation of both parties by attorneys of their choice, if desired.

Verbatim transcripts of proceedings.

A formal, written opinion submitted by the hearing officer after due deliberation.

In some instances, a variant of this formal procedure has provided, under contract, for a three-person hearing panel; one representative of the district and another from the union were added. But under all conditions, the formal process is a lengthy one; scheduling of hearings is often delayed by an inability to get all parties to the dispute together at a hearing time. Stessin pointed up how absurd a situation can become by citing one case in which there were twenty-nine witnesses, 1,936 pages of testimony, 145 exhibits, fifteen pages of briefs, and eighty-two pages of rebuttals. It is worthy of note that the arbitrator's piqued reaction to this elaborate display prompted a twenty-seven-word decision.[21] And although this situation was indeed extreme, delays, long hearings, and formalization do postpone conflict resolution and make a mockery of the American Arbitration Association's avowed intent to settle on-the-job disputes with speed, justice, and efficiency. A desire to reach these ends more expeditiously has led to a search for means of simplifying the process. One attempt that offers much promise is the "Mini-Arb" arbitration procedure.

The mini-arb procedure was adopted by the United States Steel Workers and the ten largest steel companies in 1971. Stessin reported that more than 500 companies followed suit, and also the Teamsters Union, the Long

Island Railway, a consortium of aluminum companies, and General Electric. The procedure includes the following characteristics:

Each plant facility chooses its own panel of arbitrators;

Arbitrators are jointly chosen by the union and the plant administrators from the neighborhood or area in which the plant is located;

Arbitrators serve in alphabetical order;

Lawyers are excluded from hearings (Contestants are urged to present their own cases and defenses);

Verbatim transcripts are not developed; and

Decisions are rendered orally at the end of testimony, or in the form of a one or two page statement submitted within forty-eight hours of the conclusion of the hearing.[22]

This simplified procedure is well suited to school districts that are decentralized, cost conscious, and require quick resolution of grievances in the interest of maintaining cooperative relations among staff members.

But despite its obvious advantages, the mini-arb procedure cannot be universally used in school districts. Tenure laws require formal proceedings for dismissal of tenured teachers. The California Education Code, for example, specified two types of formal hearings. If violations of statutes alone are involved, a single hearing officer is provided by the state personnel board. If questions of professional competence or ethics are at issue, the code requires a panel composed of a personnel board hearing officer, and two teachers cognizant of the specific duties of the person charged.[23] The school district may wish to resort to the benefits of the formal procedure when contract interpretation questions involve substantial amounts of money, for example, possible extended litigation about payment of back wages to an individual or a group of individuals, or other fiscal penalties imposed for failure to adhere to contract obligations.

But communication about contract provisions and grievance resolution in contract administration are remedial in the sense that they come about after the fact; they are intended to reduce conflict by interpretation of agreements already made. Some conflicts, however, could be avoided altogether if the contracting parties were fully cognizant of all alternatives available to them before the issue is resolved by insertion into the contract of a set of agreed-upon procedures. Joint committees to study an issue may provide some understanding of alternatives before contract provisions are written.

Joint Committees

Often the appointment of a joint committee, composed of board members, administrators, and employees, is a bargaining ploy used by both parties to save face in postponing a bargaining issue of lesser importance. Committees appointed under such a mandate may never meet, or meet without studying the issue, or issue a perfunctory statement just prior to the next bargaining session. Even though these activities facilitate the bargaining process, they do not contribute to the reduction of conflict. If the joint committee were to serve that end, it must search for possible alternatives to the resolution of issues that may be incorporated into contracts.

A functional joint committee is a fact-finding group; it is, in a sense, a planning group; and it is, to a degree, a research activity. Its intent is secure among board members, administrators, and union members: a clear definition of issues, tenable alternatives for joint action, and reliable data that estimate effects on all participants of the choice of each alternative. If the committee does achieve these purposes, bargaining becomes a rational selection of a mutually understood contract provision. Thus grievances and conflicts that arise after adoption could be confined to such matters as tests of validity and enforcement of compliance by intractables.

Summary

An educational organization provides an arena of conflict as well as cooperation. Much of administration is designed to assure coordination of the efforts of participants regardless of their conflicting interests, differences of definitions of terms and meaning of activities, and varied perceptions of the organization and its participants. Being an integral part of administration, the personnel department contributes to the resolution of conflicts arising from employee alienation, power struggles, status demands, recognition needs, creative impulses, failures in cooperation, advancement disagreements, differing convictions, demands for equity, and disappointment with collegial behavior. And in performing this service the personnel department is charged with the responsibility of developing collective bargaining as an integral part of the conflict resolution system.

In accepting the task of incorporating collective bargaining into the entire conflict resolution system, the personnel department is required to

Provide all employees with data concerning the advantages and disadvantages of unionism.

Use persuasion and legal remedies to assure the establishment of functional bargaining units.

Assemble all personnel and organizational data required by the bargaining parties.

Establish full cooperative relations with the district negotiator.

Strengthen the adversarial position of the negotiator by securing substitutes to keep the schools in operation in the event of a strike.

Provide the district negotiator with the projections of organizational consequences of different union proposals.

Assist in the administration of the contract once it is written.

In accepting the task of contract administration, the personnel department is required to

Develop a communication system to give each board member, administrator, and employee an opportunity to study the provisions of a current contract.

Administer a grievance system.

Assist joint committees of the board, administrators, and union representatives to study alternatives for incorporation of specified agreements in contracts.

Notes

1. *National Labor Relations Board* v. *Jones and Laughlin Steel Corporation*, 301 U.S. (1937).
2. *Congressional Record*, 93 (1947):3834-3840.
3. Lawrence Stessin, "Expedited Arbitration: Less Grief Over Grievances," *Harvard Business Review* 55 (1977):128-134.
4. Cyril Sofer, *Organizations in Theory and Practice* (New York: Basic Books, 1972), p. 344.
5. Brooks Adams, *The Theory of Social Revolutions* (New York: Macmillan, 1914).
6. Lorraine McDonnell and Anthony Pascal, *Organized Teachers in American Schools* (Santa Monica, Calif.: The Rand Corporation, 1979), pp. 45-48.
7. Edward L. Suntrup, "New Dimensions in Sunshine Bargaining," *Personnel Journal* 58 (1979):157-159.

8. California Government Code, Title 1. Division 4, Chapter 10.7, Section 3547 a-e.

9. Suntrup, "Sunshine Bargaining," p. 159.

10. *Congressional Record*, pp. 3834-3840.

11. William E. Fulmer, "When Employees Want to Oust Their Union," *Harvard Business Review* 56 (1978):163-170.

12. California Government Code, Title 1, Division 4, Chapter 10.7, Section 3545 a, b.

13. Bruce S. Cooper, "Middle Management Unionization in Education," *Administrator's Notebook* 23 (1975):2-3.

14. Ronald L. Miller, "Preparations for Negotiations," *Personnel Journal* 57 (1978):36-39.

15. Education Commission of the States, "Public Employee Collective Bargaining Laws Affecting Education in 32 States," *Phi Delta Kappan* 60 (1979):473.

16. McDonnell and Pascal, *Organized Teachers*, pp. 89-91.

17. California Government Code, Title 1, Division 4, Chapter 10.7, Section 3549.

18. Peter A. Veglahn, "Making the Grievance Procedure Work," *Personnel Journal* 56 (1977):122-123.

19. *Agreement between the Board of Education of the School District of the City of Detroit and the Detroit Federation of Teachers, Local 231, American Federation of Teachers, AFL-CIO.* For the period of September 18, 1967, to July 1, 1969.

20. H.T. Wellington and R.K. Winters, Jr., "The Limits of Collective Bargaining in Public Employment," *Yale Law Review* 78 (1968-1969):1108.

21. Stessin, "Expedited Arbitration," pp. 128-134.

22. Ibid. Used with the permission of the *Harvard Business Review.*

23. California Education Code, Chapter 361, Section 13413.

9 Compensation

The question of compensation is an important issue to personnel administration because compensation often determines (1) the candidate's willingness to choose an employer, (2) the kinds and intensity of organizational conflicts over payment equity, and (3) the willingness of employees to attend to problems of personal welfare. This point of view is most often expressed by those who subscribe to the social systems theories of administration. It is different from scientific administration adherents, who viewed compensation as the sole employee motivation, and it is different from the school human relations theorists' policies, who belived in equal salaries for all employees displaying the same number of college credits and years of experience. Adherents of social systems administration place first emphasis on self-fulfillment in employee motivation—as has been shown throughout the presentation in prior chapters of alternatives in personnel practice. But the necessity to compete with other organizations operating with the same biases requires attention to the maintenance of competitive salaries.

Competitive Salaries

It is evident that recruiting is facilitated if the district's salaries are competitive with others that recruit the same personnel. Indeed, the adoption of a competitive salary structure eliminated salary as a factor of choice, thus allowing the candidate to choose a position using self-fulfillment criteria. But a comparison of gross salaries paid by different districts is simplistic—and may be self-defeating. Gross salaries often have different purchasing power in different districts.

District Differences in Purchasing Power

Costs of living differ in geographical locations. The Bureau of Labor Statistics listed the All Items, Urban Consumers Price Indexes, as follows:

All cities on December 1, 1978 . . . 202.9 (1967 = 100)

Highest: Houston, Texas . . . 219.7

Lowest: Scranton, Pennsylvania . . . 197.1

Most Frequent: Boston, Milwaukee, Buffalo, St. Louis, Philadelphia . . . 199 + .[1]

A comparison of gross salaries, therefore, has little meaning unless the differences in purchasing power have been recognized and used to adjust them to comparable status. But for all districts, projections into the following year of even comparable salaries require some consideration of current inflation rates.

If one district whose salaries are being used in the comparison has anticipated a year ahead of time a specified inflation rate and has incorporated it into its gross salaries—a persistent union demand—then its salaries cannot be compared to those of a district that has waited to determine the prior year's inflation rate before making salary adjustments. Generally, it is unlikely for a public school district to have made adjustments for inflation during the year, although this is a common practice in business and industrial payment procedures. Public school income, being tax generated, is determined in a yearly cycle.

But even the display of a comparable salary may not serve to secure candidates for a school district. Other factors that may be crucial in attracting candidates must be considered.

Community Amenities

As noted in chapter 3 in discussing recruitment, the presence of the following community amenities may attract individuals to an employer:

A favorable climate.

Cultural opportunities (for example, theaters, symphonies, libraries, public lectures, or museums).

Opportunities for graduate study.

The district's reputation.

The presence of these amenities, to those who value them, may, in fact, be sufficient to enable an employer to pay less than a comparable salary and still maintain an ample supply of candidates. The reverse, of course, is equally possible; the absence of these amenities may require a district to pay more than a comparable salary to maintain a supply of candidates. But even if salaries are comparable, and the amenities are normally attractive, the factor of income supplements in the form of tax-free employee benefits may tip the scales in favor of an employer.

Employee Benefits

School district employers across the country are rapidly adopting the private sector wage and salary policies of providing tax-free benefits as a part of compensation. Although a later section of this chapter will discuss this sensitive issue in greater detail, suffice it to say that the Chamber of Commerce of the United States reported that, in 1977, 36.7 percent of the payroll expenditures of manufacturing and nonmanufacturing companies were expended for fourteen different types of employee benefits, as follows:

Pensions;

Disability and health insurance;

Dental care;

Life insurance;

Unemployment insurance;

Sick leave;

Vacations;

Other leaves (e.g., military, personal, jury duty, etc.)

Employee education;

Separation pay;

Moving expense;

Employee discounts;

Legal services; and

Food services.[2]

Rosow, a former assistant secretary for labor, pointed out that pension costs alone constituted 40 percent of New York City's annual payroll and that the U.S. government's employee benefit costs were 31 percent of the total federal payroll.[3]

But comparability in income, amenities, and benefits may be partially offset by the district's claims to an employee's free time. Many teachers use free time—both during the school year and the summer—to earn supplementary income.

Supplementary Incomes

All teaching is really a part-time occupation; teachers normally work 180 days per year and have eighty free days, excluding holidays. Full-time work, at least in industry, means that private sector employees work 250 days and have ten free days, excluding holidays. The National Education Association reported that in 1975-76, nearly one-third of the men (29.9 percent) and one of six of all teachers (15.9 percent) used free time to generate income. During the summer months, the NEA figures showed these earnings to amount to $1,502. Yet many teachers chose not to use summer vacation time for earnings; 33.2 percent used it for travel and 27.7 percent for purposes other than work, study, or travel.[4] Another source of supplementary income is extra pay for extra duties during school sessions.

The National Education Association reported that, in the 1975-76 school year, one of four teachers (24.5 percent) spent an average of 9.6 hours per week on extra, compensated duties. The average was ten hours per week in secondary, and nine in elementary schools. The teachers were asked to add these hours to a thirty-six-hour week (36.3), to which were then added teaching tasks of eight and one-half hours for lesson preparation, study, grading papers, and the preparation of instructional materials. When the extra duty time was added, it cumulated to a work week for teachers of 54.4 hours in secondary and 51.4 hours in elementary schools.[5] Clearly, both on- and off-duty incomes can present significant additions to gross incomes; they must be considered when making salary comparisons.

Thus, with or without the other factors discussed, the need for comparable salaries to attract, and sometimes help to retain, employees for an organization seems significant. But the ability of the district to maintain salary levels depends, in part, on the public recognition of the value of the services it purchases. Similarly, the ability of the district to retain personnel depends, in part, on its ability to resolve conflicts that arise over equity in assignments. It is part of the personnel department's responsibilities to assist in the resolution of both these problems of equity.

Compensation Equity

Although the term fairness is difficult to define—other than in a context of sports—it does present specific dimensions in each arena in which it is used. In educational employee compensation, fairness involves the public (that is, how are the children doing in school?) and the employees (that is, faculty and staff who want equal payment for equal work). Wage and salary administration—a complex task shared by the personnel department, administrators, the employee organizations, and the board of education—consists to a great extent in designing ways fairly to resolve the conflicts arising from these two major thrusts for equity. The personnel department's efforts to resolve the public's concern for getting a fair and reasonably skillful effort in the classroom in exchange for salaries requires cooperation from the profession. It is a dimension of cooperation that has never been very extensive; it may be said that preoccupation with collective bargaining issues has diminished it further for the moment.

Public Concepts of Compensation Equity

There is no doubt that the public wants to "get it's money's worth" in paying teachers' salaries. But the public has demonstrated a notable caution in enforcing its demands by a support of the single salary schedule for over half a century (fifty-six years, to be precise). Only recent state laws, which raised the requirements for entry into teaching to five years of collegiate preparation, have caused the indentification of teaching with other professions. It also caused reexamination of compensation equity.

Professional Compensation

If the day will dawn that teachers are identified with professionals, along with lawyers, doctors, nurses, and engineers, it is safe to predict that, eventually, the criteria for determining reasonable skill and effort will be the same as for those professions. In chapter 6, discussing performance appraisal, professionals were cited as needing to "exercise good judgment . . . due care and diligence . . . perform as a reasonably prudent and carefully trained person . . . use requisite skill. . . ."[6] The willingness of the public to utilize these criteria may never come about for teachers, unless the joint effort of the district and the profession can provide operational definitions of skills, good judgment, diligence, and training that will "stick."

It is, then, the members of the profession who expect the public to provide funds to finance their concept of equitable salaries who must also identify the skills required to reach educational ends. As in most other professions, the level of compensation here must be persistently determined by the public's recognition of the quality or scarcity of essential skills. And the profession can expect an inevitable result of skill identification: public demand that the more skillful members receive a higher level of compensation than the less skillful. A reasonable, and acceptable, exception to the public's perception of skill level compensation may be a form of maintenance pay (automatic raises) during a probationary period designed to give a beginning teacher an opportunity to develop reasonable competency. But thrusting the burden of identification of teaching skills on members of the profession may be a frustrating process unless the school district facilitates it by its personnel actions.

Some of the prior chapters have discussed and recommended personnel actions that may assist the profession in the skills identification process. Notably, assignments may identify tasks, the range of skills needed to complete each, and their order of difficulty in development. Performance appraisal, also, may not only assist each teacher in identifying skills possessed, but the recommended coaching procedure may provide a means of securing staff consensus concerning needed skills. Reinforcement of these assignment and evaluation policies may be obtained by a salary policy to direct attention to the relations between scarce skills and levels of compensation provided. Designed to incorporate the achievement classifications recommended in chapter 7, discussing human resource development, the levels of pay may be identified with (1) minimal skills (required for task acceptance), (2) required skills (for continuation), (3) desired skills (for all experienced teachers), (4) outstanding skills (for coaching of other teachers), and (5) exceptional skills (for instruction of evaluation coaches). The form such a salary structure might take is suggested in figure 9-1.

The adoption of a salary structure related to skills, however, will not satisfy another aspect of the public's concept of equity. Most of the public is well aware—along with most teachers—that different teaching assignments do not require the same effort, level of skill, or knowledge. This perception produces doubt whether the differentiation of salaries only on such factors as number of courses completed and years of service is very realistic. It is the basic steel industry that is using the best-known current plan for coping with pay for positions of unequal effort: job evaluation.[7] Patton reported that employee, union, and organization satisfaction with job evaluation procedures for establishing salary sequences for each different kind of position was close to 90 percent.[8] The public doubt about the equity of existing procedures goes back to years of experience with techniques for determining the worth of an assignment to the organization. This kind of stratification was first used in civil service classifications of the late nineteenth century.[9]

Job Evaluation

In the nearly ninety years of experimental development of techniques to determine the worth of an assignment to the organization, techniques have varied from a simple procedure of rating to a complicated process which used the semantic differential technique in employee surveys. Some that have most often been tried are (1) classification (U.S. Civil Service Commission), (2) factor comparison,[10] (3) various point systems in which numerical values were assigned to different job factors,[11] and (4) the extent of unsupervised work (recommended by Elliott Jacques).[12] Often two or

SKILLS	STRUCTURE	SALARY
MINIMUM SKILLS:	Required for entry level	Level 1 $
REQUIRED SKILLS FOR CONTINUATION:	Automatic	Level 2 $ 3 $ 4 $ 5 $
DESIRED SKILLS: (for all experienced teachers)	Proof of skill	Level 6 $
OUTSTANDING SKILLS: (for evaluating coaches)	Proof of skill	Level 7 $
EXCEPTIONAL SKILLS: (instruction of evaluation coaches)	Proof of skill	Level 8 $

Figure 9-1. Suggested Salary Structure according to Achievement Classifications

more of these systems were used in combination. One strategy that seemed to arrive at some sense of equity in compensation was discussed by Beatty and Schneier. They reported that a ranking procedure using paired comparisons yielded results almost identical with more complex, and less easily understood, procedures.[13]

In using the ranking system recommended by Beatty and Schneier, it is essential that each assignment be identified in terms of goals to be reached, tasks assigned, skills required, and interactions desired. Using these data and a paired comparison technique (that is, identification of top and bottom positions in the list, then the ones nearest to top and bottom, and a continuation of the process until all positions are ranked), multiple raters, including representatives of individuals holding the positions, were asked to rank all positions in the organization. Decision criteria included knowledge required, level of skill needed, time required to complete the tasks assigned, hazards of the assignment, and numbers of qualified candidates willing to join the organization for that work. Using an average ranking, and identifying clusters of similar positions, it becomes possible to determine the relative worth of each position to the organization. The rankings thus derived enable the organization to establish, within the resources available, a salary structure for each type of assignment.

The adoption of this procedure may be well advised to increase the public's confidence in the fairness of compensation policies. For the employees, monetary incentives based on relative value of the task at hand may encourage persistence in several areas, notably (1) in difficult assignments, (2) in the development of rarer skills for challenging appointments, (3) in the acceptance of hazardous duties, and (4) in the acceptance of positions in the district rather than moving to other organizations. But the public's concern for professional behavior and equity in pay for unequal assignments is accompanied by a concern for maintaining salaries in a period of inflation.

Cost-of-Living Salary Adjustment: The Public's Concepts

Probably because members of the public have experienced inflation firsthand, they have demonstrated a willingness to increase teachers' salaries to compensate for skyrocketing prices. Adjustments have been made in different ways by different districts. In the eight-year period of 1967-68 through 1975-76, the purchasing power of teachers' salaries increased nationwide by 1.2 percent. In twenty-one states, real incomes declined. Only two of nine regions, Mid-East and the Rocky Mountains, showed an increase in real income of more than 2 percent.[14] These figures reflect the attempt on the part of school districts to keep up with an inflation spiral that, according to the National Education Association, nearly doubled the average salary of classroom teachers during the period, increasing it from $6,253 in 1966 to $12,005 in 1976.[15] These data seem to support a conclusion that the public has accepted the necessity of cost-of-living adjustments, but that the procedures for making them vary in effectiveness.

School districts, attempting to achieve a more orderly system of adjusting salaries according to changes in the Consumer Price Index, may encounter difficulties inherent in their own political independence. Indeed, more uniformity would require somewhat comparable action by over 16,000 semi-independent school districts. And, of course, each has its own unique problems of competing for scarce public tax funds with other governmental units; besides, the Consumer Price Indexes (CPIs) differ among diverse geographical areas. School districts—unlike other organizations of similar magnitude in numbers of employees—find it difficult to make adjustments during the school year because taxes providing school monies are levied only once per year. Manufacturing and nonmanufacturing union contracts that call for adjustments of a one-cent hourly wage increase for each .03 (or .04) rise in the CPI are difficult to use in school districts. And the American Telephone and Telegraph policy of increasing employees' weekly salaries by $.50 plus .6 percent of the total for each 1 percent rise in the CPI is equally unusable.[16] For public school teachers, reliance on bargaining (negotiations) and the public's sympathy with the procedure may prove to be the only tenable alternative.

But the incorporation of these innovations into policies which assure the public of compensation fairness—and which foster its willingness to maintain salary levels—may, of itself, be inadequate to motivate teachers, at least until their views of what constitutes compensation equity are taken into account.

Teachers' Concepts of Compensation Equity

Teachers, to some extent, share with the public a conviction that equity in compensation includes (1) competitive salaries (usually the first proof offered to substantiate salary raise demands by union negotiators), (2) professional salaries (even though they may disagree about the structure), (3) an obligation of the administrators to equalize work loads of different assignments (unwilling to concede its impossibility, union leaders often vigorously oppose job evaluation even if union members endorse it after it is adopted), and (4) cost-of-living adjustments. Teachers may disagree about the manner in which these problems of equity can be resolved, although most are aware of the need to resolve them in a manner that will foster continuing public support. But there are other problems of equity that have not, as yet, become public concerns. And one of the most persistent is what would seem to be the obvious need to provide year-round salaries for heads of families.

Year-round Incomes

The fact that year-round income presents a problem arises, logically enough, from the part-time nature of teacher employment. As noted earlier, characteristically, the problem has been met by teachers, in part, by conversion of free time into income by one in three men teachers and one in six of all teachers. It has also been met, in part, during school sessions, by assumption of extra, compensated duties by one of every four teachers. The perception that compensation is inequitable is further enhanced by the use of free time, by one of three teachers, for travel, and by another third for no activity.

It would seem that the job-seeking routine during May and June of each year is an onerous chore for heads of families. Some have attempted to deal with the problem by various methods: (1) starting their own businesses; (2) developing a skilled trade (carpentry, masonry, and so on); (3) returning to the same employer as a summer substitute for employees on vacation; or (4) whenever possible, teaching summer school classes. In addition, assumption of extra duties during school sessions, intended to alleviate accute financial distress, does, in effect, present another set of frustrations. The acceptance of a work week in excess of fifty hours (noted in this chapter as 54.4 hours in secondary and 51.4 hours in elementary schools) in a culture in which 39.5 hours per weekly assignment is most common, often requires the extra duty worker to brush off requests by colleagues, family members, and friends to participate in their activities. If, for reasons of a sense of obligation or other causes, the teacher accedes to their requests, he may find it necessary to postpone, ignore, or give scant attention to a substantial portion of his regular assignment. In either case, the maintenance of extra income is frustrating and certainly encourages a perception of compensation inequity.

Two changes in compensation policy may be suggested to resolve the equity problem for heads of families: (1) a year-round salary can be made available if redesign of assignments includes year-round positions for which heads of families are qualified—if the summer sessions do not provide opportunities to develop year-round assignments, there is much academic (if not teaching) work that can be done between sessions; (2) a second action may assist those who take on extra duties during the school year. Recognizing the cultural endorsement of a 39.5 hour week, and bowing to the inevitable frustrations of the over-scheduled employee, it may be more productive to include what is now termed "extra duties" into the regular assignments of the staff. This action will become more feasible if the single salary schedule is replaced by the multiple schedule, one that is based on job evaluations, because obviously the concept of extra pay under the latter is untenable. Equally untenable, for the reasons that relate to the multiple schedule emphasis on skill, is the single salary schedule payments for credits earned.

Costs of Inservice Education

The single salary schedule practice of rewarding the accumulation of credits by advancement to a higher pay bracket for the completion of fifteen credits seems patently unfair in terms of cost-benefits. The advancement to a higher bracket has traditionally meant a yearly raise of $150-$250 (a median of $200). Using an average expectancy of ten years in the profession, less two years to earn the credits, and the median value of the column increase, the net income gain to the teacher for gaining fifteen credits proves to be $1,600 (more, of course, if tenure exceeds ten years). The tuition cost to the teacher, if it is assumed that three credits will have been earned in district-operated workshops, can be $1,440 in a medium-cost private university, and $600 in the average graduate school of a public university. Added to these tuition costs are the book purchases, travel expenditures, and food costs—all expended in one or two years and recovered in eight. It is possible to envision many situations in which the cost of gaining the fifteen credits exceeds the benefits to be gained in the form of additional salary.

Even under the single salary schedule (despite its apparent dual pay implications), school districts have tended to resolve the equity problem by providing sabbatical leave salaries and reimbursing teachers for tuition costs. The Educational Research Service reported that, in 1975-76, 60.3 percent of all districts (93.3 percent of districts expending $1,300 or more per year on each pupil) provided all or some portions of the teacher's salary while on sabbatical leave. It reported that one in four districts (26.1 percent) reimbursed teachers for tuition costs.[17] However, if the multiple salary system with its focus on skills (instead of credits earned) were to be used, the bonus of the double payment will no longer be there; the costs of inservice development can be assumed by the district as the price of goal achievement—although the assumption of inservice costs by the district incurs, of course, the risk that there may be no return on the investment. This is a type of risk characteristic also of maintenance payments.

Maintenance Payments

The policy of giving automatic raises during the probationary period has been noted previously in this chapter as a problem of equity in salaries. Other maintenance pay policies may be described as follows:

> Continuation of salary level even though the employee is assigned to duties requiring less skill than previous assignments. This may be done to retain skilled individuals expected to be needed at a later date; to maintain support for an individual handicapped by illness, accident, age, or skill obsolescence; or to support an employee until he has time to find another employer.
>
> Longevity payments to individuals at strategic intervals of continued employment (for example, fifteen years of service, twenty years, or twenty-five years). This policy is justified by motivation to remain with the organization.

The resolution of salary equity problems constitutes a reasonable policymaking process (save, perhaps, for the emotional commitment of teachers to the single salary schedule). The motivational potential of salary policies can be identified, alternatives can be perceived and tested, and tenable practices can be established. The process can be simplified by relating salary to tasks, skills, and goal accomplishment, clearly daily concerns of teachers. But tax-free benefits, which have become a major factor of compensation, are not daily concerns of teachers. Walker pointed out that they are not generally noticed by the employee, if provided solely by the employer, until they are used; the employee is satisfied by their mere existence.[18] As a result, the development of rational policies for their inclusion in compensation suffer from lack of attention to purpose, tests of alternative procedures, and inattention to eventual costs.

Employee Benefits

The motivations leading an educational employer to devote a large proportion of the salary budget to employee benefits may be diverse, but they are identifiable as follows:

> Pensions: designed to encourage each employee to save while working to live comfortably in retirement.
>
> Disability: designed to provide support in the event of impairment that makes continuation at work impossible.

Health care: designed to maintain physical and dental health to facilitate continuous and vigorous effort at work.

Sick leaves: designed to facilitate absence, without salary penalties, from contact with students when ill.

Other leaves: designed to enable employees to be with families at times of crises; to attend to business affairs not possible during working hours; to serve on juries, meet military obligations, or serve the public as a consultant; to participate in religious ceremonies not recognized as holidays by the school district; and to enable women teachers to bear children without penalty.

Life insurance: designed to provide a hedge against family suffering when its prime support is removed.

Legal services: designed to encourage the making of wills; and provide assistance in adoptions, purchases and sales of property, separation agreements, divorce or annulment, alimony, probate proceedings, consumer complaints, repossessions, evictions, tax audits, juvenile offenses—all of which may become problems for teachers.

It stands to reason that the fulfillment of these goals has frequently been frustrated, in some instances by the procedures adopted, in others by irresponsible acts of some employees who abused their intent (for example, leaves).

Further discussion of benefit programs will group together the categories that are normally mutually inclusive. The first of these is the examination of disability in conjunction with the pension plan because some provisions for disability are usually included in the retirement program.

Pension and Disability Systems

The chief characteristic of 1979 pension funds, both public and private, is the extent of unfunded obligations in each. They represent a vacuum created by persistent inflation which has caused major increases in wages and salaries. Because pension payments normally consist of a proportion of the last year's salary, or an average of the three highest years' salaries, obligations—in relation to higher salaries—exceed the income of accumulated deposits made from lower salaries. In many organizations, the extent of these unfunded obligations may be staggering.

Ehrbar, in writing about unfunded pension obligations, reported that, in 1976, ten of the top 100 companies of *Fortune* magazine's list of 500 had unfunded pension obligations equal to a third or more of their net worth.

He cited the Lockheed Aircraft Company as having vested pension benefits of $1.3 billion, an amount equal to 82 percent of all of its assets. The unfunded portion was $276 million, 66 percent more than the market value of the company's stock.[19] In a supplement to the Ehrbar article, the editors of *Fortune* pointed out that the cities of Boston, Detroit, Los Angeles, and Jacksonville, Florida, had unfunded pension obligations in excess of their total municipal debt. Similarly, the General Accounting Office of the U.S. government in 1976 reported, according to the editors of *Fortune*, unfunded pension liabilities in the federal Civil Service System of $107 billion (salary increases during the past three years may well have pushed that figure much higher). Indeed, the large 1978 increases in contribution rates aimed at stabilizing the Social Security System may prove to be inadequate to fund its payments in the early 1980s unless the following assumptions prove to be true: (1) the inflation rate can be reduced to 4 percent by 1982, (2) the unemployment rate diminishes to 5 percent by 1981, (3) real wages can be increased by 16 percent by 1984, and (4) the national birth rate per woman increases from 1.7 to 2.1 by 1985.[20] The California legislature in 1972 recognized the unfunded problem in the State Teachers Retirement System (STRS). It attempted to meet the problem by establishing a yearly contribution rate of 16 percent of each teacher's salary—to be paid half by the district and half by the teacher. It also agreed to contribute $135 million per year until 2002 to reduce unfunded obligations.[21] Despite this drastic action, the unfunded obligations of STRS in California were estimated in 1978 to be in excess of $5 billion. It is fair to conclude that the problem of unfunded pension obligations requires remedies not now in use if the goals of the pension system are to be reached.

Some remedies are more acceptable than others, some are more feasible, and some are completely untried. A brief review may shed some light on alternatives that are open, as follows:

> Restriction of participation to career employees: this could be accomplished by postponing entry into the system until some designated age—say thirty—and postponing vesting of pension rights in deposits for another five years. This policy, if adopted in schools, would substantially exclude the teacher who entered the profession at twenty-two and remained in it for no more than ten years.
>
> Fund the present system from public tax revenues: the unfunded pension obligations in state teachers' retirement systems are legally a lien against the general revenues of the state. But insistence on that lien being paid encounters all the usual difficulties of securing regular appropriations from the legislatures or coping with their being shifted to the local school districts. In either event, in times of scarce revenues, the lien may be met by reduction in appropriations for current expenditures.

Lay off a part of future pension obligations to the Social Security System by joining it: the Educational Research Service reported that, in 1975-76, 59.8 percent of all school districts surveyed had adopted this option.[22]

Increase contribution rates: this is, of course, the option chosen by the California legislature in 1972 and the Congress in stabilizing the Social Security System in 1978. As has been demonstrated in both actions, there is a tendency to underestimate the need by legislative groups. It tends to reduce current incomes and produces demands for additional salaries which exacerbate the problem.

Make participation in the pension system voluntary: this may be a welcome policy for families in which two members are both contributing to the pension fund—a not unusual situation among married teachers. But unrestricted freedom to participate obviously defeats the intent of the district in its endorsement of pension policies.

It is reasonable to predict that no one of these alternatives will prove to be the touchstone for the solution of the problem; all are likely to be adopted, modified, and changed in the search for a solution. This prediction may also apply to disability payments which are normally a division of the retirement system.

Disability income is often related closely to retirement. In the State Teachers Retirement System of California, for example, teachers claiming disability must have been active members of STRS with five years of credited service. The claim must have been approved by a review panel composed of a physician, a vocational consultant, an attorney, a contributing member of STRS, and an STRS staff member. The claimant must have proved a physical or mental condition of long, continued, and indefinite duration. If proved, and under the age of sixty, the claimant receives half of the average salary paid during the highest-paid twelve consecutive months of the thirty-six preceding the onset of the disability. A 10 percent increase of that amount is given for each dependent child under eighteen, or twenty-two if the dependent is still in school. But at age sixty, the regular retirement is calculated; the disabled teacher then receives the retirement salary or the disability payment, whichever is higher.[23] The systems in other states coordinated with Social Security rely on its disability payments. In either event, disability shares with the retirement system all the problems of support.

Disability and pensions, however, is but one of the benefit programs that need review. The leave policies of school districts have, in many cases, become operating handicaps.

Leave Policies

Leave credits, which accumulate easily, often are considered by employees to be vested rights that can be used at will, regardless of the district's intent in providing them. For an example, the cost of substitutes in New York City schools in 1971-72 was $71.5 million.[24] For another, the Educational Research Service pointed out that, in 1975-76, more than four-fifths of a national sample of school districts (83.3 percent) provided teachers with ten to nineteen days of sick leave per year. Nearly half (45.5 percent) permitted an unlimited accumulation of unused days. Nearly two-thirds (60.6 percent) granted an average of three days per year for personal leave. A fifth (18.5 percent) granted an average of three days per year for religious leaves, but a third of them (31.3 percent) charged such leaves to sick leave.[25] The problem is no different in business and industrial employment; Jucius reported that, in the 1960s, as much as 50 percent of all absenteeism was attributed to sickness, or alleged sickness.[26] A study of teacher absenteeism in Indiana, in 1975-76, found that in 86 percent of all school districts absenteeism had increased each year for the prior five years, despite declining enrollments and numbers of teachers.[27] Teachers come to believe that the rights are vested by the twin practices of (1) allowing unlimited accumulation of leave credits and (2) paying them at severence or retirement for unused portions of the accumulation. The Educational Research Service reported that, in 1976, a third of all school districts granted separation or retirement bonus pay in this way, and that half of them reserved it for retirement only.[28] It appears reasonable here to suggest that, because absenteeism forces the district to pay twice for the service on the day of absence, a reduction in absenteeism is calculated not only to improve instruction, but to reduce its costs.

Since leave control systems (for example, prior permission, submission of doctors' statements, or telephone checks at the absentee's home on the day of absence) are neither very effective in results nor inexpensive in execution, remedies for excess absenteeism may need to be based on policy changes. Some that may assist follow:

Limit accumulated leaves to ten or fifteen working days: this procedure may prove to be more acceptable if employees are provided opportunities to participate in an employee paid income guarantee group insurance plan.

Accept maternity leave as sick leave for the period of confinement and recovery: maternity leaves for subsequent child care may be treated as uncompensated leaves of absences.

Provide a block of three days per year, in addition to sick leave, for compassionate and personal leaves: if not used in a given year, they may be allowed to expire at the end of the school year.

Provide public duty leaves after prior proof of need: these should be provided outside of sick leaves.

Make religious leaves available outside of sick leaves: a limit of three days per year may be provided and they may be allowed to expire at the end of the year, if unused.

If separation pay is provided at severance or retirement, provide funds from general salary accounts without reference to leaves.

Any of these measures, if adopted, may serve not only to emphasize district purposes in leaves, but also to decrease the costs of absenteeism. But it is possible to decrease even the legitimate costs of sick leaves if districts examine closely their purposes in providing or supporting health- and dental-care benefits.

Health- and Dental-Care Benefits

Some statistics are in order here before a discussion can be attempted. More than half (63.2 percent) of all districts surveyed by the Educational Research Service in 1975-76 paid the full premium for group hospitalization for teachers; more than half of those (35.0 percent) paid full premiums for family coverage. More than half (61.9 percent) paid the full premium for major medical-surgical group insurance for teachers; more than half of those (35.2 percent) paid the full premium for family coverage. One-fourth (25 percent) paid the full premium for dental care for teachers; more than half of those (17.7 percent) paid part or all of the premium for family coverage. But only a small proportion (4.3 percent) of the districts paid part or all of the premiums for vision-care group insurance; but half of those (2.2 percent) paid part or all of the premiums for family coverage.[29] This extensive benefit coverage is being provided concomitant with vaulting medical-care costs. The Federal Index of Medical Care Costs increased from 120.6 in 1970 to 168.6 in 1975.[30] Since 1975, the yearly rate of increase has been in double-digit figures. It would seem that this is an appropriate time to examine the extent to which these expenditures are achieving the ends sought.

The original intent of the employer in establishing health-care benefits was to encourage prompt and unimpeded attention to health which, if left untended, might cause absences from work, work at less than complete effectiveness, or death. Employees were expected to use the services thus provided to assure early detection of difficulties and remediation. Lofty though its intent, this health-maintenance purpose has not been fully realized. Requiring insightful employee participation, the program's preventive aspect has often been lost in obscurity. Some found the paper work involved in the claims procedure to be burdensome. A part of the problem may well have been the choice of an insurance-based system that required detailed proof of eligibility and treatment. But the purposes of the program cannot be faulted; hence the procedures will have to be simplified because the personal involvement of the employee is essential.

Due to the fact that insurance companies require such attention to detail in proof of eligibility and treatment, a partial solution may be a substitution of a health-maintenance type of medical service, commonly referred to as HMO. Gumbiner pointed out its advantages by citing a program in Guam. In 1972, when the HMO had enlisted half of the 100,000 Guamese in the program, there was a critical hospital bed shortage. Three years later, the hospitals were running at one-half occupancy. During this three-year period the rates for coverage increased only six-tenths of a percent each year.[31] Gumbiner gave much credit to the preventive aspects of the HMO care. He added that smaller groups may also create an HMO and referred to the R.J. Reynolds Industries of Winston-Salem, North Carolina, an organization of 10,000 employees. But under either type of service (HMO or insurance), it would seem incumbent on the employer to mount a constant educational campaign with employees in order to keep them aware of the intent of the health-maintenance plan. But, clearly, the HMO simplicity of providing service on presentation of a valid identification card beats the drawn-out task of insurance claiming. On the other hand, group life insurance claims do not share with health insurance the same burdensome routine.

Group Life Insurance

Almost half (44 percent) of the districts of the national sample studied by the Educational Research Service in 1976 provided full payment for group life insurance for teachers.[32] This would appear to present an uncomplicated addition to compensation. The employee whose spouse is covered under another program, however, or a family that has developed an independent insurance program with specific goals may find this diversion of salary to be a less productive investment than another alternative. As a result, there are advantages to making participation in the group life insurance program voluntary. If a teacher chooses not to participate, equity requires that the annual premium, which would otherwise be provided, be paid to the non-participant in the form of cash or other benefits. And this same policy may need to be used in providing what is the newest benefit program currently prevalent both in public and private employment—legal services.

Legal Services

The *Personnel Journal* reported that nonmanufacturing and manufacturing contracts with personnel included, in 1978, provisions for legal services for more than 3 million employees. More than 3,500 prepaid legal plans were filed with the Employee Retirement Security Administration (ERISA) in 1977.[33] No secure data are available concerning the extent of prepaid legal services in school contracts, but the road has been paved for their inclusion. The Educational Research Service reported that, in 1976, nearly two-fifths of school districts (39.2 percent) provided professional liability insurance for at least some teachers. Over a third (36.9 percent) paid the full premiums.[34] The prepaid legal cost in the private sector ranged, depending on the type of service included, from as little as $4.00 per month per employee to $20.00 per month for family coverage.[35]

Summary

Compensation determines, in part, the choice of an employer, the kinds of intensity of organizational conflicts over payment equity, and the willingness of employees to attend to problems of personal welfare. In using compensation to attract employees, a competitive salary is essential. But comparing gross salaries is self-defeating.

Gross salaries may be adjusted, however, to be comparable if the following are taken into account:

Differences in purchasing power.

Community amenities.

Employee benefits.

Supplementary incomes.

Even if adjusted and competitive at the time of comparison, they may not be maintained unless the public considers them fair.

The fair teacher's salary, in the public view, is a professional salary paid to teachers whose skills are identifiable, and known. A fair salary requires larger payments to the more skilled, more burdened, better prepared, more jeopardized, and more in demand. And the public is willing to provide salaries that are adjusted upward with inflation rates. Even though teachers may disagree about the manner of securing equity, they generally support the public concept of salary equity. They do, however, recognize other problems of equity not now public concerns.

In addition to the now public concerns, teachers who are heads of families perceive the need for year-round salaries. In view of benefits to be received, and current pay practices, teachers recognize the fairness of districts' paying the costs of inservice education. They recognize the fairness of maintaining salaries during probation, and while being transferred to another employer. They endorse longevity payments as incentives to remain with the same employer. But most teachers fail to recognize the district's compensation intent in the provision of employee benefits.

Employee benefits have become a major cost in teacher salary budgets, but each is malfunctioning to some degree. Inflationary pressures have created large, unfunded obligations in most pension systems. Leave policies have proved to be incentives for absenteeism. Health-maintenance programs have not only become very expensive, but they fail to achieve preventive goals intended. Group life insurance programs have proved to be too universal. This may also prove to be the case with legal services.

Notes

1. Bureau of National Affairs, *1979 Briefing Sessions on Collective Bargaining: Workbook* (Washington, D.C.: The Bureau, 1979), p. 36.
2. Ibid., p. 62.
3. Jerome Rosow, "Public Sector Pay and Productivity," *Harvard Business Review* 55 (1977):6-7.
4. National Education Association, *Status of the American Public School Teacher: 1975-1976* (Washington, D.C.: The Association, 1977), p. 43.
5. Ibid., p. 56.
6. John W. Wade, "The Attorney's Liability for Negligence," *Professional Negligence* (Nashville, Tenn.: Williams Printing Company, 1960), p. 224; Ted M. Warshafsky, "Approaches to Hospital Negligence," *Case and Comment* 5 (1960):12.
7. J. Stieber, *The Steel Industry Wage Structure* (Cambridge, Mass.: Harvard University Press, 1959).
8. J.H. Patton, *Job Evaluation in Practice: Some Survey Findings*, Management Report No. 54 (New York: American Management Association, 1961), pp. 73-77.
9. Craig E. Schneier and Richard W. Beatty, *Personnel Administration Today* (Menlo Park, Calif.: Addison-Wesley, 1978), p. 434.
10. P.M. Edwards, "Statistical Methods in Job Evaluation," *Advanced Management Journal* 33 (1968):158-163.

11. Robert W. Gilmour, *Industrial Wage and Salary Control* (New York: John Wiley and Sons, 1956), pp. 64-105.

12. Elliott Jacques, *Time Span Handbook* (London: Heinerman, 1964).

13. Schneier and Beatty, *Personnel Administration*, p. 438.

14. Richard A. Musemsche and Sam Adams, "The Rise and Fall of Teachers Salaries: A Nine Region Survey," *Phi Delta Kappan* 58 (1977):479-481.

15. National Education Association, *Status of the American Teacher: 1975-1976*, p. 8.

16. Bureau of National Affairs, *Workbook: 1979*, p. 34.

17. Educational Research Service, *Fringe Benefits for Teachers: 1975-1976* (Washington, D.C.: The Service, 1976), p. 23.

18. Samuel C. Walker, "Improving Cost and Motivational Effectiveness of Employee Benefits," *Personnel Journal* 56 (1977):570-572.

19. A.F. Ehrbar, "Those Pension Plans Are Even Weaker Than You Think," *Fortune* 96 (1977):104.

20. Daniel Seligman, "Keeping Up," *Fortune* 97 (1978):52.

21. California State Teachers Retirement System, *Information Booklet* (Sacramento, Calif.: STRS, 1976), p. 6.

22. Educational Research Service, *Fringe Benefits: 1975-1976*, p. v.

23. California State Teachers Retirement System, *Booklet*, pp. 14-15.

24. Peggy C. Elliott and Donald C. Manlove, "The Cost of Skyrocketing Teacher Absenteeism," *Phi Delta Kappan* 59 (1978):269-271.

25. Educational Research Service, *Fringe Benefits: 1975-1976*, p. 22.

26. Michael J. Jucius, *Personnel Management*, 7th ed. (Homewood, Ill.: Richard D. Irwin, Inc., 1971).

27. Elliott and Manlove, "Teacher Absenteeism," pp. 269-271.

28. Educational Research Service, *Fringe Benefits: 1975-1976*, p. 24.

29. Ibid., pp. 25-27.

30. U.S. Bureau of the Census, *Statistical Abstract of the United States: 1976*, 97th ed. (Washington, D.C.: U.S. Government Printing Office, 1976), p. 72.

31. Robert Gumbiner, "Selection of a Health Maintenance Organization," *Personnel Journal* 57 (1978):444-446.

32. Educational Research Service, *Fringe Benefits: 1975-1976*, p. 27.

33. "Editor to Reader," *Personnel Journal* 57 (1978):534-536.

34. Educational Research Service, *Fringe Benefits: 1975-1976*, p. 27.

35. "Editor to Reader," *Personnel Journal,* p. 31.

Epilogue: The Dialogue of Change

Many of the recommendations of this text may appear difficult to adopt; some may arouse defensive reactions by teachers and administrators alike. Others may be accepted too quickly without understanding. The following dialogue may clarify some of the major issues in the interest of their rational consideration.

Question: The text defined goals as a product of a dynamic community consensus of educational beliefs. How can a consensus be achieved, developed, and maintained in the kind of diverse metropolitan society you describe?

Answer: The communication technology is in place. Elihu Katz, as early as 1957, after a study of group behavior, pointed out that a community contains many primary (face-to-face) groups in which there is an opinion molder to whom others of the group turn for interpretations of meanings of communications they have received.[1] For school districts, the school advisory group has become commonplace, because it was required by the government in schools receiving Title I federal monies. It may be assumed that advisory committee members are opinion molders. Thus, if they are challenged to resolve with members of primary groups the policy issues of the metropolitan society, it becomes possible to develop and arrive at a consensus of what ought to be done educationally for each child and youth in the community.

Question: But a metropolitan community is composed of many groups that defend fiercely their religious, ethnic, or class identifications. How can these parochial interests be reconciled for common educational action?

Answer: There are three procedures available to the educational leader to effect such a reconciliation. The first is a communication program that raises the concept of how community is perceived to a level of consciousness. As Havighurst pointed out in 1968, the community exists; it may merely be unperceived.[2] And we do cooperate in metropolitan areas in providing for health and safety, culture, recreation, welfare, work, leisure, transportation, communication media, and political cooperation. If our current interdependence on the accessibility of these services is perceived, it would seem but a short step to recognition of a similar interdependence in education. And some metropolitan areas have already taken this step—some voluntarily, from a recognition of need, for example, Hartford, Connecticut, and Nashville, Tennessee. Others have taken the step reluctantly, under court orders to secure integration, for example, Wilmington, Delaware; Louisville, Kentucky; and Indianapolis, Indiana. The establishment of a metropolitan educational authority may not yield immediate cooperation of self-conscious, parochial groups, but it provides a framework within which a metropolitan consensus may be developed, a consensus that may, slowly, secure a recognition of a common destiny. If, because of this undesirable parochialism around us, the achievement of a full community consensus turns out to be light-years away, a third procedure may be explored as an interim necessity. There is, likely, in each community within the large metropolitan center, a community consensus, each with somewhat different goals and procedures. Each may require decentralization according to the consensus achieved. But even decentralization is to be done with the recognition that some educational beliefs are common to all decentralized areas.

Question: But even if consensus is reached and common goals are valued by the community and the educational staff, how can a system of administration be changed to reflect it?

Answer: An administrative system grows; it is not adopted. It develops, much like a living entity, as each policy is instituted that is designed to respond to the multiple political, economic, and social pressures exerted on the schools. If these multiple decisions—made over time and even by different personnel—display a common intent, they may at some point be said to be a system. But if it is the intent to build a system, then responsiveness, patience, and consistency are essential. One purpose of this text was to develop a model that values these characteristics and thereby serves as a beacon. But, as was discussed in the preface, the purpose of administration is to coordinate many, often conflicting, organizational elements so that they are able to operate as a unity. It is, therefore, self-defeating to initiate administrative procedures that require those who must work together to behave in ways they can neither justify nor value. In other words, each step in building an administrative system must have the following elements: it must represent the resolution of a problem of cooperation fully understood by all concerned, and the choice of an alternative among several previously tested. It must also be instituted with an intent to evaluate.

Question: It sounds like a very slow process that offers little promise that the personnel services soon will be devoted to human resource development. How can that be guaranteed?

Answer: It can't be guaranteed. But because, under this system, the personnel department is in the forefront of the staff in responding to the political, economic, and social pressures of the metropolitan community, a concern for achieving educational goals directs attention at once to the persons most responsible for reaching them—the teachers. Interestingly, it is not its new role that brings about this needed change. No, the new role is rather the result of its classic role—it is in its classic role of recruiting, developing, and retaining teachers that the personnel department meets the problem of organizational adaption first. And because of this, it is fair to conclude that the personnel department will also be the first element of administration to change its policies, recommending concomitant changes in the policies of other units that will facilitate its work.

Question: Granted that the personnel department may be the locus of administrative change, what influence can it have in securing professional behavior from teachers?

Answer: The personnel department remains confined to its traditional administrative role of insisting that skills be identified for recruitment, that evaluation provide opportunities for exchange of expertise, and that advancement opportunities be provided by classification of skills. This does not suggest that the problem is, therefore, insoluble. But the personnel department's responsiveness is not only directed at the external pressures of the society. Within the classroom, almost casually, certainly regularly, a teacher may face a most frustrating experience, that is, a teaching-learning problem with the students without the foggiest notion about what to do. The first impulse is to turn to another teacher who may, or may not, have been able to resolve the problem in the past. But, taking advantage of this almost reflex action, the profession has an obligation to secure from its members their accumulated experience and make it available to all. It seems unarguable that this procedure will provide insight concerning essential skills that will be valued by other members of the profession. Surely, as classroom populations become more diverse, this experience is multiplied a thousand times, increasing the need for available experience. Its urgency is emphasized by transfers that charge teachers with instruction of pupils from subcultures they neither know nor understand. It is a procedure crucial to teachers, whose only preparation has been in sheltered practice-teaching classes. It is underscored by pupil transiency, which provides classrooms with a national cross-section of students. And it is made imperative by mainstreaming of special education students. Student diversity in classrooms can be said to be the greatest challenge to professional development that teachers have encountered in this century.

Question: Granting that the political, economic, and social pressures of today will eventually require professional behavior of teachers, what assurance is there that the public will be willing to support a profession exhibiting these scarce skills?

Answer: In a sense, it is necessary to return for the answers to the responses to the first two questions—support depends on the value the community places on the work of teachers. Community needs that are satisfied from tax funds are both tangible—streets, sewers, storm drains, fire departments, police departments, and government—and intangible—education, libraries, museums. Each will receive support from the taxpayers to the extent it has relative value to the others. If the taxpayer suspects that anyone can teach—anyone, that is, who meets a state license requirement—then pay will be provided in that range of competition. If, on the other hand, the taxpayer understands the scarcity of teaching skills—and recognizes the most difficult as comparable to the skills of another profession highly valued—he will likely be willing to lift competition to that higher skill structure. Clearly, salary levels depend not only on the willingness of the profession to identify the skills of teaching, but to demonstrate their effectiveness in reaching valued educational goals.

Notes

1. Elihu Katz, "The Two-Step Flow of Communications," *Public Opinion Quarterly* 21 (1957):61-78.

2. Daniel Levine and Robert J. Havighurst, "Social Systems of a Metropolitan Area," in *Metropolitanism: Its Challenge to Education*, 67th Yearbook of the National Society for the Study of Education (Chicago: University of Chicago Press, 1968), pp. 37-70.

Index

Adams, Brooks, 8, 14, 130, 144
Adams, Sam, 167
Aleamoni, Lawrence M., 96, 105
Allbrook, Robert C., 125
Allport, Gordon, 6, 14, 76
amenities (community), 40-41, 148
Anderson, Robert H., 38, 53
applications (weighted), 45-46
appraisal of performance, 91-95; as means of role fulfillment, 93-95; as measure of efficiency, 91-92; as measure of group compatibility, 92-93
appraisal procedures, 96-99; choosing evaluators, 97-98; evaluation as coaching, 98-99; reporting evaluations, 99; timing of evaluations, 96-97
assessment centers, 60-61
assignments, 73-88; under human relations, 75-79; under scientific administration; 73-75; under social systems coordination, 79-88

Bakke, E. Dwight, 108, 125
bargaining domains, 138
Batt, William L., Jr., 114, 125
Beatty, Richard W., 60, 71, 105, 153, 166, 167
Bennis, Warren, 77, 89
bimodal neoscientific and neohumanism administration, 8
Bion, W.R., 60
Bray, D.W., 60, 71
Broudy, Harry S., 17, 30, 97, 100, 105
Bureau of National Affairs, 167
Burke, Edmund, 24

Caldwell, Robert M. 125
Carlson, Richard O., 62, 72
Cartwright, Dorwin, 6, 14
change, 170-172; in administrative systems, 170; in human resource development, 171; in public support, 172; in teacher behavior, 171-172
collective bargaining, 131-138; and data collection, 134-136; and duties of personnel department, 137-138; and process of, 131; and strike communications, 137; and substitutes, 136-137; and sunshine laws, 131-132; and unit formation, 132-134
collegiality, 75-85; as cooperative goal-seeking, 83-85; as developer of mediocrity, 75; as pure democracy, 78-79
community cooperation, 109-113; and allocating responsibilities to individuals, 112-113; and allocating responsibilities to units, 111; and defining role of school, 109-111
competencies (CBTE), 17, 33-34
conflict resolution, 75-88; by management fiat, 75; by open discussion, 79; by value consensus, 85-88
conflicts in organizations, 127-131; resolution in schools, 130-131; types, 127
consensus, 169-170; and communication technology, 169; and decentralization, 170; and parochial interests, 167
consumer price indexes, 147-148
contract administration, 138-143; and advisory arbitration, 140-141; and binding arbitration, 141-142; and grievance procedures, 139-140; and interpretation of agreements, 138-139; and joint committees, 143
Cooper, Bruce S., 134, 145
Coser, Lewis, 85, 89
Cubberley, Ellwood P., 5
Curtis, William W., 33, 52

Darcy, C. Michael, 17, 30
Davis, Russell C., 28, 31
Dempsey, Richard A., 38, 53
Dewey, John, 6
Dyer, Frank J., 59, 71

Educational Research Service, 157, 161, 163, 164, 167
Edwards, P.M., 166
Ehrbar, A.F., 159-160, 167
Elliott, Peggy C., 167
employee benefits, 149-165; extent in the private sector, 149; health and dental care, 163-164; leaves, 162-163; legal services, 165; life insurance, 164; pensions and disability, 159-161; purposes of, 158-159
England, G.W., 45, 53
evaluation, 93-95; as aid to role fulfillment, 93-94; and collegial opportunity, 94-95; and encouragement of creativity, 95; as means of developing self-evaluation, 95; as professional obligation, 94; as reinforcement process, 94
evaluation obstacles, 99-104; demands for accountability, 100-102; dismissal appraisals, 104; diversity of educational practices, 99-100; gratuitous evaluations, 102-104

Fawcett, Claude W., 18, 30, 36-37, 53, 118-119
fishbowl bargaining, 131-132
Flanagan, John C., 96, 105
Follett, Mary Parker, 79, 85, 89
Foulkes, Fred K., 1, 10, 13, 14
French, Wendell, 1, 13, 59, 71
Fulmer, William E., 133, 145
fusion, 108

Gardner, John W., 15, 30
Gilmour, Robert W., 167
Goodlad, John I., 34, 38, 53
Greene, Jay, 13
grievances, 139-142; clinical process of, 139-140; legalistic process of, 140-142
Griggs vs. *The Duke Power Company,* 59
Gumbiner, Robert, 164, 167
Gunderson, Robert G., 76, 89
Gyllenhammar, Pehr G., 7, 14

Halpin, Andrew, 115, 125
Havighurst, Robert J., 169, 172
Health Maintenance Organization (HMO), 164
Herzberg, Frederick, 69, 72, 80, 89
Higgins, James M., 42, 53
human relations: and collective bargaining, 128-129; and group compatibility, 55; and group development, 107-108; and group membership, 75; and group selection, 34; interpretation of as democracy, 6; and peer evaluation, 92-93; and planning a group process, 15
human resource development, 109-124; and goal determination, 109-113; and organizational participation, 113-117; and skill development, 117-122; and reinforcement of behavior, 122-124

interviews, "gating", 47. *See also* patterned interview

Jaques, Elliott, 152, 167
Johns, Roe L., 8, 14
Johnson, Henry C., Jr., 101, 106
Jucius, Michael J., 162, 167

Katz, Elihu, 169, 172
Kay, Patricia M., 33, 53
Kluckhohn, Clyde, 9, 14

Land, Edwin H., 10
Lawrence, P.R., 111, 125
Levine, Daniel, 172
Lewin, Kurt, 6, 76, 89
Likert, Rensis, 114-115, 125
Logue, John, 113, 114, 125
Lorsch, J.W., 111, 125
Lortie, Dan, 123, 125

McDonnell, Lorraine, 144
McIsaac, George S., 114, 125
McLellan, D. Daniel, 21, 31
McMurry, Robert N., 19, 30, 37, 53, 56, 61, 63, 71, 72
Maher, J.R., 48, 53
Manlove, Donald C., 167
Maslow, Abraham, 80, 89
Massarik, Fred, 115, 125
Mausner, Bernard, 69, 72, 89
Melcher, Robert D., 109, 111, 125
Metcalf, H.C., 89
Miles, Matthew W., 9, 14, 86, 89, 115, 125
Miller, Ronald L., 134-135, 145
mini-arb procedures, 141-142
Moore, Harold, 4
Morgan, Henry M., 1, 10, 14
Morphet, Edgar L., 8, 14
motivation, 63-69, 73-81; employee as entrepreneur, 73-74; employee as goal seeker, 80-81; employee as group member, 76-77; Herzberg's dissatisfiers, 69; Herzberg's satisfiers, 69; McMurry's needs categories, 63
Murray, Henry A., 60
Musemeche, Richard A., 167

National Education Association, 39, 53, 150, 154, 166
National Labor Relations Board vs. Jones and Laughlin Steel Corporation (1937), 128, 144
National Training Laboratory, 76
neohuman relations, 7-8
neoscientific management, 7

participation in organizations, 113-117; codetermination (European concept), 113-114; maintaining a favorable cooperative environment, 116-117; role fulfillment (American concept), 114-115
Pascal, Anthony, 144
patterned interview, 67-70; interviewers' techniques in, 70; response interpretation in, 68-70; setting of, 67
Patton, J.H.,152, 166
personnel actions, 35-39; audits of teachers' skills, 36-37; determining personnel needs, 38-39; maximizing use of scarce personnel resources, 37-38; unit task audits, 35-36

personnel services, 1-12; in business and industry, 1, 2; development in public schools, 1, 3-5, 6; employee relations, 12; in government, 2; and human resource development, 12; and organizational planning, 10; and service to administrators, 11
planning and the personnel department, 15-29; contingencies, 28; in emergencies, 28-29; information to be supplied, 15-24; long-range planning, 26-28; periodic planning, 25-26
Pointer, V.V.N., 17, 30
Pottinger, J. Stanley, 43, 53
Project Interaction, 109-110

Rand Corporation, 131, 134, 137-138
records of personnel, 16-24; and educational beliefs, 20-22; and group maintenance behavior, 29-32; and interactions with other groups, 24; and interactions within work group, 23-24; and participation in record maintenance, 16; and skills of teaching, 16-18; and work habits, 18-20
recruitment, 34-51; and advertising, 40; and affirmative action, 42-45; and cooperation with professionals, 41; determination of needs, 34-39; evaluation of sources of supply, 41-42; personnel exchanges between districts, 50-51; relations with placement officers, 39-40; screening of applicants, 45-48; personnel transfers, 48-50; and voluntary applications, 40-41
reinforcement of behavior, 123-124; by earning freedom for professional choices, 124; by evaluation, 123-124; by joint goal-striving with students, 123
Reller, Theodore L., 8, 14
Reuther, Walter, 129
Rodda Act (1974), 132, 133, 138
Rokeach, Milton J., 20, 21, 30, 31
role definition, 74-83; as fixed segment of work plan, 74; as goal achievement, 81-83; as group dynamics, 77-78
Rosner, Benjamin, 33, 53
Rosow, Jerome, 149, 166
Roth, Robert A., 33-34, 53

salary comparisons, 147-150; and benefits, 149, community amenities, 148; and consumer price indexes, 147-148; and supplementary incomes, 149-150
salary equity (employees' views), 155-158; extent of agreement with public's views, 155; and inservice education support, 157; and maintenance payments, 158; and year-round incomes, 156-157
salary equity (the public's views), 151-155; and cost of living adjustments, 154-155; and job evaluation, 152-154; and professional salaries, 151-152
salary structure, 153
Schmuck, Richard A., 86, 89
Schneier, C.E., 26, 31, 60, 71, 105, 153, 166, 167
scholastic records, 56-57; activity reports, 57; informal confirmation, 57; transcripts, 56
Schulz, Charles, 104, 106
Schutz, William C., 19, 30, 62, 72
scientific administration: Cubberley's adaptation for schools, 5; efficiency standards of, 91-92; employee as entrepreneur, 73-75; interchangeability of personnel, 33; negotiations with personnel, 128; planning as engineering, 15; and selection to determine efficiency, 55; and self-development, 107
Scott, W.D., 59
selection, 55-70; and confirmation of work habits, 61-66; and departmental purposes, 55; and patterened interview, 67-70; reports, 70; and skills confirmation, 59-61; and validation of records, 55-59
selection reports: purpose, 70; elements of, 70
selection tests, 59
Selznick, Philip, 21, 31, 81, 89
Sergiovanni, Thomas J., 117, 122-123, 125
Sheehan, Daniel S., 96, 105
Shepard, Herbert A., 77, 89
skill development, 117-122; as qualification for administration, 120-122; as system of advancement, 117-120
Smith, Rodney F., Jr., 38, 53
Snyderman, Barbara, 69, 72, 89
social systems coordination: and choosing work alternatives, 55; and conflict resolution as administration, 130-131; problems of, 7-9; and employee as goal seeker, 79-88; and human resource development, 108-109; and planning for use of human capital, 15-24; and role fulfillment, 93-95; and search for colleagues, 34-39
Sofer, Cyril, 19, 23, 30, 59, 71, 80, 86, 89, 92, 102, 105, 106, 111, 125, 129, 144
Stessin, Lawrence, 141, 142, 144, 145
Stieber, J., 166
Stoddard, George D., 38, 53
strikes, 136-137, 145
Suntrup, Edward L., 144, 145

Taft-Hartley Act (1947), 129, 133
Taft, Robert A., 128
Tannenbaum, Robert, 115, 125
Taylor, Frederick W., 73, 74, 75, 89
teacher centers, 120, 125
telephone checks, 56-58; purposes of, 56; questions, 57-58
Tuchman, Barbara, 26, 31

Urwick, Lionel, 89

Veglahn, Peter A., 139, 145

Wade, John W., 101, 106, 166
Wagner Act (1935), 128, 129
Walker, Samuel C., 158, 167
Warshafsky, Ted M., 101, 106, 166
Webster, E.C., 47, 53
Weinberg, Edgar, 114, 125
Wellington, H.T., 145
Wilson, Alfred P., 33, 53
Winters, R.K., Jr., 145
work habits, 62-66; and aspirations, 62; career-bound, 62; and competitivenesss, 65-66; and curiosity, 65; and desire to serve, 66; and need for income, 63; and perfectionism, 66; place-bound, 62; power-seeking, 64-65; and problem rejection, 62; security needs, 64; and status behavior, 64; of women, 62-63
work sampling, 59-60

Young, Stanley, 9, 14

Zander, Alvin, 6, 14

About the Author

Claude W. Fawcett is a professor in the Graduate School of Education, University of California, Los Angeles. Prior to coming to UCLA he was the Educational Director for the Western Division of the National Association of Manufacturers. He is the author of a book entitled *School Personnel Administration* (1964). He has contributed chapters to two National Society for the Study of Education *Yearbooks* on vocational education and metropolitanism. He has also contributed a chapter to each of the three editions of *Foundations of Education*.